How
Academic
Leadership
Works

Robert Birnbaum

How
Academic
Leadership
Works

Understanding
Success and Failure
in the College Presidency

 Jossey-Bass Publishers
San Francisco

For sales outside the United States, contact Maxwell Macmillan International Publishing Group, 866 Third Avenue, New York, New York 10022.

Manufactured in the United States of America.

The paper used in this book is acid-free and meets the State of California requirements for recycled paper (50 percent recycled waste, including 10 percent postconsumer waste), which are the strictest guidelines for recycled paper currently in use in the United States.

Library of Congress Cataloging-in-Publication Data

Birnbaum, Robert.
  How academic leadership works : understanding success and failure in the college presidency / Robert Birnbaum.
      p.   cm. — (The Jossey-Bass higher and adult education series)
  Includes bibliographical references and index.
  ISBN 1-55542-466-X
  1. College presidents—United States.   2. College administrators—United States.   3. Leadership.   I. Title.   II. Series.
LB2341.B479 1992
378.1'11—dc20   92-8766
                                                                          CIP

This publication was prepared partially with funding from the Office of Educational Research and Improvement, U.S. Department of Education. However, the opinions expressed herein do not necessarily reflect the position or policy of OERI/ED, and no official endorsement by OERI/ED should be inferred.

FIRST EDITION
HB Printing   10 9 8 7 6 5 4 3 2   *Code 9260*

The Jossey-Bass
Higher and Adult Education Series

Contents

Part Three: Improving Academic Leadership

Preface

This book is about leadership in the academic community and how college presidents and other campus leaders affect their institutions. Those who write about higher education, as well as those who study organizations in general, have disagreed about the extent to which leaders — especially those who fill the role of chief officer — make a difference. On the one hand, the traditional models of leadership that pervade our culture are built on the belief that leadership is the single most critical component of organizational success. On the other hand, it has been suggested that organizational constraints and common elements in experience and training make leaders essentially interchangeable and that an organization's performance is more influenced by its structure, history, culture, and environment and the socialization of its members. In *How Academic Leadership Works,* I hope to contribute to this important discussion.

This book is also about institutional renewal. Many leaders help improve their colleges, and leave them a bit better than they found them. But a few leaders are able to do even more; they help college participants reaffirm their values, replenish their energy and commitment, and find satisfaction in their collective enterprise. As we shall see, college presidents influence this process of renewal by constantly reminding people of the values they cherish and helping them act in ways consistent with their beliefs.

How Academic Leadership Works is based on data collected by the Institutional Leadership Project (ILP), a five-year longitudinal study of how college and university presidents and other leaders interact and communicate, assess their own and others' effectiveness, establish goals, learn, transmit values, and make sense of the complex and dynamic organizations in which they work. The emphasis on interaction and communication is deliberate, because leadership in higher education rests on a fundamental expectation that authority will be shared. Governance requires the interaction of many groups, and each group has one or more leaders. Hence academic leadership, of necessity, is the responsibility of many people.

Here I approach the reciprocal relationships between institutions, leadership, and values from a cultural and interpretive perspective that is consistent with the views expressed in *How Colleges Work* (Birnbaum, 1988a, p. 2): "The important thing about colleges and universities is not the choices that administrators are presumed to make but the agreement people reach about the nature of reality. People create organizations as they come over time to agree that certain aspects of the environment are more important and that some kinds of interaction are more sensible than others. These agreements coalesce in institutional cultures that exert profound influence over what people see, the interpretations they make, and how they behave."

Some academic leaders who think of leadership primarily as planning or decision making find to their dismay that they have little influence over the values or commitment of their followers. Because of this, they may fail to help their institutions to the extent that they otherwise might. However, the data collected in this project provide no basis for accepting the recurrent proclamation that there is a leadership "crisis" in higher education. It is true that few college presidents today enjoy the reputation of the giants of a century ago. But the plaintive query, Where have all the great leaders of the past gone? has an elementary answer: They are dead, along with the simpler times in which formal leaders could wield unbridled power to get what they wanted. In today's world of greater participation, shared influence, conflicting constituencies, and assorted other complexities, heeding the current vogue of calls for charismatic presidents who can transform their institutions would be more likely to lead to campus disruption than to constructive change.

This book suggests a more modest, but still hopeful, view of what leaders can hope to achieve. Most people in campus leadership positions do well in the complex and confusing academic environment, and their stewardship has generally supported their institution's ultimate objectives. Nevertheless, they can often do somewhat better, and I offer suggestions for achieving that improvement.

This study of college leaders is empirically grounded and displays primarily qualitative data in two ways. First, it presents the comments of institutional leaders, allowing them to speak for themselves as individuals. Unless otherwise identified, all quotations in this book are taken from ILP interviews. Second, it uses data reduction processes (Miles and Huberman, 1984) to organize interview data and prepare them for collective quantitative analysis. Generalizations drawn from these data are presented throughout the book; some of the analyses appear in Resource C. Detailed descriptions of methodology have been presented in the various ILP publications cited throughout the book; such descriptions are minimized here, since the book is aimed at practitioners as well as researchers. For the same reason, I do not offer any extended discussion of the literature of leadership in higher education. Such a discussion can be found in *Making Sense of Administrative Leadership: The "L" Word in Higher Education* (Bensimon, Neumann, and Birnbaum, 1989), which analyzes the usefulness of existing leadership research for understanding colleges and universities.

The ILP has been among the most comprehensive studies ever conducted on leadership in higher education. To date, in addition to this book, the ILP has produced fifty-one books, monographs, chapters, papers, and research reports, which are available either from the Center for Higher Education Governance and Leadership (formerly the National Center for Postsecondary Governance and Finance) at the University of Maryland, College Park, or in the books or journals in question. These works are listed in Resource D.

Audience

Although *How Academic Leadership Works* focuses attention on college presidents, the book is neither exclusively about them nor exclusively for them. Leadership involves interaction and reciprocity, the distinction between leader and follower is often arbitrary, and institutional renewal requires the committed involvement of sizable numbers of people who have a legitimate claim to leadership. Those in formal leadership positions on campus, including trustee officers, senior administrators, and heads of institutionwide faculty organizations, will find themselves in these pages. The research findings and conclusions are as much about them as about college presidents.

Overview of the Contents

This book is divided into three parts. Part One introduces the ideas about leadership that form the basis of the study. Chapter One presents a view of leadership as a cultural and interpretive phenomenon. It emphasizes the ways in which presidents and constituents develop shared understandings of equivocal environments and ambiguous internal processes. The ILP is the first study to give attention to how academic leaders think and the "frames" through which they make sense of their institutions and their own performance. Chapter Two uses the ILP research findings to analyze five leadership myths about transformation, vision, charisma, distance, and personal styles and traits — myths that may mislead presidents and others as they carry out their roles. It also considers three mysteries about teams, experience, and gender that have implications for the future study and practice of academic leadership. Chapter Three proposes a definition of good leadership based on constituent support and assesses the extent to which the characteristics of institutions, the backgrounds and experiences of their presidents, and the ways in which the presidents think are related to whether those presidents are considered good leaders. This chapter also introduces several ideas about leadership processes that form the conceptual basis of the research. Some of the terms used, such as *cognitive complexity,* have only recently been introduced in the study of higher education and will be new to many readers.

Part Two considers the relationship between presidents and their several constituencies, in particular the faculty, and how these interactions can promote institutional renewal. Chapter Four examines how presidents are assessed by their faculties and traces changes in the relationship between leaders and their constituents from the time the presidential search begins to the time a president leaves office. It focuses attention on a phenomenon previously suggested but never studied — presidents' tendency to lose faculty support over the span of their term in office. Chapter Five paints a longitudinal portrait of three presidential career paths — identified here as those of the "exemplary president," the "modal president," and the "failed president" — that reflect the level of faculty support for a president. These paths define the constraints on presidential influence and show why most presidents can help their college to improve only marginally, while a few can help fashion its renewal. Of course, institutional renewal is not the work of one person, and Chapter Six analyzes the ways in which leadership can be effectively shared on campuses. The chapter gives particular attention to leadership by those in leadership roles, by individuals all through the organization who provide leadership without title or formal constituency, and by governance organizations such as senates. This dispersal of leadership is not only an essential precondition for renewal; it is also the reason colleges can improve even when their presidents are not effective. Chapter Seven uses the ideas of the three presidential paths and dispersed leadership in presenting two case studies of institutions that were renewed. The cases suggest that renewal may take place under a variety of institutional conditions and circumstances but that the roles that presidents, faculty, and others play in the process have certain features in common.

Part Three summarizes some of the concepts illuminated by the study and suggests what can be done to improve institutional leadership. Chapter Eight integrates the research findings to offer an understanding of leadership as it presents itself in academic environments. It shows how presidential paths are related to "instrumental" and "interpretive" leadership in different ways and discusses organizational factors that can either substitute for, neutralize, or enhance presidential leadership. Finally, Chapter Nine makes recommendations for what presidents and other leaders in higher education can do to improve their colleges. We are not now — and almost certainly never will be — able to prescribe presidential actions that will assure an exemplary career and college renewal. But the research findings do suggest what presidents can do to prevent undue erosion of the support on which their influence depends.

The book includes four resources. Resource A lists the thirty-two study institutions that were the research sites for the ILP. These colleges and universities were selected to reflect the great diversity in the major sectors of American higher education. Resource B includes an example of the interview protocols used by ILP researchers to ensure that data collected by several researchers at different times and sites would be comparable. Resource C presents summaries of some of the ILP data, and the relationships between them, that were used in developing the ideas in this book. These data include characteristics of the study institutions, the backgrounds of their presidents, presidential modes of thought, the level of faculty support enjoyed by the presidents, and several dimensions of campus change. Resource D lists the publications of the ILP to date, and the publishers from which copies may be obtained.

Acknowledgments

Many of the ideas that went into this book, like the Institutional Leadership Project itself, were developed with two colleagues working collaboratively with me at Teachers College, Columbia University. Estela M. Bensimon, now at Pennyslvania State University, and Anna Neumann, now at Michigan State University, served as research associates and assistant directors on the project. They did most of the campus interviews during the initial visits in 1986–87, and the three of us shared (with Barbara Lee of Rutgers University) the follow-up visits two years later in 1988–89. We all participated actively in the preparation of the data analyses and papers that defined some of our basic scholarly concepts and provided the intellectual foundation for this volume. We functioned as a team in developing ideas, writing papers, providing editorial support for each other's work, and otherwise sharing the labor that a five-year study requires. The manuscript benefited greatly from their comments and criticisms on several drafts.

The support of many individuals and groups was critical to the success of the ILP. The research itself was conducted under the aegis of the National Center for Postsecondary Governance and Finance, whose executive offices were at the University of Maryland, College Park. The National Center, and the ILP, were funded through a five-year grant from the Office of Educational Research and Improvement (OERI), Office of Education. Two program officers, Salvatore Corrallo and Jeffrey Gilmore, contributed suggestions and helpful criticism. (The National Center has now been reconstituted as the Center for Postsecondary Governance and Leadership.)

In addition to the resources of OERI, the project was fortunate in attracting support from the Lilly Endowment and from the Teachers Insurance and Annuity Association/College Retirement Equities Fund (TIAA/CREF) that made it possible to investigate important aspects of leadership in greater depth than would otherwise have been possible. Peggy Heim of TIAA/CREF was a good friend who provided us with moral support and encouragement.

The structure and procedures of the ILP were guided in their early phases by a technical advisory committee of distinguished scholars and practitioners. Chaired by the late Howard Bowen, the committee included Elias Blake, Jr., Shirley Browning, Kim Cameron, Madeleine F. Green, Anita M. Pampusch, and Piedad F. Robertson. Joseph F. Kauffman served as senior research consultant to the project.

Several national associations agreed to be identified as sponsors of the project, and some have disseminated ILP findings to their members through newsletters and related publications. Sponsors included the American Council on Education, the American Association of Community and Junior Colleges, the American Association of State Colleges and Universities, the Association of American Universities, the Council of Independent Colleges, the National Association for Equal Opportunity in Higher Education, and the National Association of Independent Colleges and Universities.

Colleagues from other institutions, including Ellen Earle Chaffee, Barbara Lee, and William G. Tierney, joined us at several points in our research to participate in the interviewing process and worked with us in analyzing portions of our data. We were also fortunate to have the administrative support of Eleanor Fujita, who kept the ILP functioning smoothly and at the same time became a research colleague through the completion of her dissertation. Her doctoral study, like that of Janet Judy Lathrop, made an important contribution to this book.

Several colleagues, including Richard P. Chait, Richard M. Cyert, Eleanor Fujita, Madeleine F. Green, Joseph F. Kauffman, William G. Tierney, and several anonymous reviewers, read the manuscript in draft form and made important contributions to both substance and style. The extensive scholarly and editorial suggestions of Wagner Thielens, Jr., were of particular value in making the book more coherent and readable. Julia Bates, Dyanne Lyon, Robert (Skip) Myers, Merrill Schwartz, Monika Springer Schnell, and Terry Zacker, all doctoral students in the higher education program at the University of Maryland, College Park, assisted in the analysis of the data reported in Chapter Seven and in other ways made helpful comments and suggestions. I am indebted to the copyeditor, Elspeth MacHattie, for her careful, thoughtful work.

My greatest debt, though, is to the trustees, presidents, administrators, and faculty leaders at thirty-two institutions who permitted ILP researchers to visit and took time from other pressing business to talk to us about their institutions, their colleagues, and themselves. The administration and faculty of Westchester Community College, in the same spirit, participated in a pilot study of ILP materials. I hope that the scholarly contributions of the ILP will repay their generosity in part, and that our interpretations of what they have said will give them new insight into their own professional endeavors.

After five years of intensive work, I have found, as have almost all those who have studied this topic in the past, that many basic questions about leadership remain unanswered and are perhaps unanswerable. My reading in the literature of leadership and my research experiences over the past several years have convinced me that research cannot provide *answers* to the puzzles of leadership. However, good research can help us think of interesting new *questions* and develop new vocabularies that can help us talk about leadership in more useful ways and move us toward a deeper and more complex understanding of it.

I hope this book will serve those purposes. I accept full responsibility for sins of omission and commission, hoping that my scholarly successors will profit from what I have done and will correct my errors.

College Park, Maryland   Robert Birnbaum
June 1992

The Author

Robert Birnbaum is professor of higher education at the University of Maryland, College Park. He has also served on the higher education faculty at the University of Miami and in the Department of Higher and Adult Education at Teachers College, Columbia University, where he was also chair. He is a former president of the Association for the Study of Higher Education and was a recipient in 1990 of its annual Research Achievement Award.

Birnbaum has held administrative positions as vice-chancellor at the City University of New York, vice-chancellor of the New Jersey Department of Higher Education, and chancellor of the University of Wisconsin, Oshkosh. He has also served as a member of the board of trustees of Montclair State College.

He is the author, coauthor, or editor of seven books and monographs in addition to *How Academic Leadership Works,* and his research findings appear regularly in higher education journals. From 1985 to 1990, he was director of the Institutional Leadership Project at Teachers College, Columbia University.

Birnbaum received his B.A. degree (1958) in psychology from the University of Rochester and his M.A. (1965) and Ed.D. (1967) degrees in higher education from Teachers College, Columbia University.

How
Academic
Leadership
Works

PART ONE

The Nature of Academic Leadership

CHAPTER 1

Understanding Leadership

There is a constant temptation to say more than we know about leadership in higher education. It is usually not too hard to explain retrospectively why an organization responded to a leader in a certain way and to use the outcomes to frame guidelines for prospective leaders. But outcomes in one setting may not be replicable in others, and an explanation that in hindsight appears obvious may not necessarily be true. This book is in part the report of an empirical study of higher education leadership. Its findings and conclusions are based on data collected by the Institutional Leadership Project (ILP), an intensive five-year examination of college presidents and other academic leaders. But in addition to analyzing what we *do* know about leadership, the book is also in large measure an inquiry into the limits of what we *can* know about it. Leadership is defined not only by what leaders do but also and even more importantly by the ways in which potential followers think about leadership, interpret a leader's behavior, and come over time to develop shared explanations for the causes and outcomes of ambiguous events. We can appreciate why leadership will never be understood with certainty through illustrations of the complexities of leadership as they are experienced in the real world. Consider some potential outcomes of three real-life situations encountered by the ILP. Suppose you were a college president faced with these situations

and trying to predict the potential consequences of your actions.
Which outcomes would you consider most likely?

> *Situation 1.* A new college president whose style em-
> phasized participation and delegation replaced
> an authoritarian president who had microman-
> aged the institution. In the old days, faculty had
> bypassed the administrative structure and gone
> directly to the president to get things done. The
> new president resisted micromanagement or in-
> tervention in lower-level problems and expected
> deans to make decisions. How did the faculty
> respond?

a. Faculty were pleased because the decision pro-
    cess was more regularized and involved less
    favoritism.
b. Faculty were pleased because stronger deans
    provided a more effective voice for college
    faculty in institutional decision making.
c. Faculty were displeased because they had less
    personal contact with the president.
d. Faculty were displeased because delegation
    made the president appear indecisive.

> *Situation 2.* A president asked the board to ban un-
> authorized structures on campus after the fire-
> bombing of a shanty built by students protest-
> ing the institution's investment policy. After more
> shanties were erected, the president acted to have
> them removed as a threat to student safety, and
> demonstrators protesting the removal were ar-
> rested. How did the faculty respond?

a. Faculty were pleased because protest activities
    disrupting academic activities on campus had
    been ended.
b. Faculty were pleased because potential hazards
    to student safety had been removed.

    c. Faculty were displeased because removing the shanties violated principles of freedom of expression.

    d. Faculty were displeased because they shared the students' views on the investment policy.

Situation 3. A faculty member was recommended for tenure by both a department and an ad hoc nondepartmental committee. The president rejected the recommendation on the grounds that previous actions of this faculty member had violated the freedom of expression of others. The president distributed to the campus a lengthy report summarizing the case and indicating the reasons for the decision. How did the faculty respond?

    a. Faculty were pleased because the president's action indicated that the university would not tolerate behavior that limited others' freedom of expression.

    b. Faculty were pleased because the distribution of the written report indicated that the president had treated the matter seriously and had given it careful consideration.

    c. Faculty were displeased because the president did not accept a faculty personnel recommendation based on peer review.

    d. Faculty were displeased because rejecting a tenure decision on grounds of violating freedom of expression of others itself violated the freedom of expression of the faculty member.

Clearly, in each situation you could easily construct scenarios that would make any of these outcomes appear plausible. However, you probably would not feel at all confident in predicting which was most likely to occur.

But what is ambiguous in prospect becomes less so in retrospect. There is a human tendency to remember an outcome as certain and obvious when it was not at all certain as the situation unfolded. If you were told what actually happened in each of these three scenarios, later you would be likely to think of the outcomes as inevitable and unsurprising, and even to believe incorrectly that you had accurately predicted them. The ease with which we all do this makes a relationship between leader behavior and organizational consequence seem clear and compelling. Sometimes the attribution of the effects of leaders is valid, but often it is not.

The "right answers" to the three scenarios—what actually transpired—are d, c, and b. If you answered correctly, does that mean you truly understand what outcomes leaders can expect from their actions? Perhaps. But because of the ambiguities of leadership, even accurate predictions do not necessarily provide evidence of organizational acumen. Each of these examples presented you with a highly structured situation and four alternatives, one of which was promised to be "correct"; the leaders in the real-life situations had no such structure and acted without assurance that any of these outcomes were likely. In addition, even selecting an alternative at random would yield a "correct" answer some of the time; how could you (or the president involved) know with assurance whether an accurate response was due to skill or to luck? Finally, while many people on these three campuses might agree that the outcomes described here actually occurred, not all would. In the absence of unanimity on what actually happened, or the reasons for it, whose perceptions should be accepted as accurate?

You may believe that you suffer an unfair disadvantage in this exercise in prediction; after all, the actual presidents had access to information not available to you. While that is true, this additional information might have been as much misleading as revealing. The real-life presidents would not have found it easy to separate signal from noise and would have had no way of being sure which of the many things happening at the same time were really connected in some important way to the problem and its outcome. What might appear on the surface to be a clear result of leadership on further examination might be shown to be caused by other factors. If it is so difficult to relate leader behavior to organizational consequences, why do we feel certain that leaders are so important?

Even when organizational events or outcomes are not consistent with what people have come to expect, and the causes are not clear, we still tend to attribute them to the acts of leaders. This happens because leaders are prominent and visible in many organizational activities and processes, we have a need to relate organizational events to the intended activities of others rather than to chance, and we *expect* people identified as leaders to be agents of institutional change. This tendency to attribute influence to leaders, even when it may not be objectively warranted, distorts the way we think about leadership, and obscures the actual relationship between leaders and outcomes (Phillips and Lord, 1981; Pfeffer, 1977). What we think we know about leaders may come less from careful observation of the consequences of their actions and more from imputing qualities to them based on our implicit theories of what leaders of successful organizations must be like (Meindl, Ehrlich, and Dukerich, 1985).

The Conflicting Views of Leadership Research

We still know relatively little about leadership, but it is not for lack of trying. The most encyclopedic survey of the field of leadership research (Bass, 1990) cites over 7,500 studies on the topic, and a small subset of this literature, focused on higher education, has recently been examined in an extended bibliographical essay (Bensimon, Neumann, and Birnbaum, 1989). Judged on the basis of the degree of attention given to it at least, understanding leadership appears to be important to us indeed.

Most of the writing on leadership in higher education is descriptive or prescriptive and tends either to explicitly advocate or implicitly accept that leadership — and particularly presidential leadership — is a critical component of institutional functioning and improvement. This view, however, is not held unanimously. Some observers and analysts emphasize a "strong leader" model, arguing for the importance of presidential behavior (Commission on Strengthening Presidential Leadership,

1984; Keller, 1983; Gilley, Fulmer, and Reithlingshoefer, 1986; Fisher, 1984; Whetten and Cameron, 1985). But some present a "weak leader" position, focusing attention on the environmental and organizational constraints that limit presidential discretion (Birnbaum, 1989e; Walker, 1979), and make the potent president an illusion (Cohen and March, 1974).

Data are available to support both views. One empirical study of academic organizations concluded that institutional effectiveness was closely related to the strategies of senior administrators (Cameron, 1986); the simplest explanation of this finding would be that the actions of leaders have important consequences. Another study found that some important measures of institutional functioning remained unchanged even as presidents were replaced (Birnbaum, 1989c), implying that institutional fates may not be closely related to who presidents are or what presidents do.

It is tempting, in view of these opposing positions and differing findings, to ask the question, Does leadership matter? In the real world, there is almost never a simple yes or no answer to this question. Even those who believe in the importance of leadership recognize that leaders are frequently unable to act as they would like (Kerr and Gade, 1986), and even those who posit that leadership is more symbol than substance acknowledge that leaders can make a difference under certain conditions (Cohen and March, 1974; Birnbaum, 1988a). Any comprehensive consideration of academic leadership must be able to accommodate both the strong leader and the weak leader views, because evidence suggests that while both may be incomplete, both are in some measure correct.

An Interpretive View of Leadership

Instead of asking if leadership matters, perhaps it is better to ask, Under what conditions can leaders make a difference? One very helpful approach for investigating this question is to view a college or university from a cultural and interpretive perspective. Culture in higher education has been defined as the "collective, mutually shaping patterns of norms, values, practices

"Yes, he's definitely assuming leadership. A case of the right ant in the right place at the right time, evidently."

beliefs, and assumptions that guide the behavior of individuals
and groups in an institution of higher education and provide
a frame of reference within which to interpret the meaning of
events and actions on and off campus" (Kuh and Whitt, 1988,
p. 13). There is a growing belief that culture and leadership
are closely related. Schein (1985, p. 2), for example, has suggested that "the only thing of real importance that leaders do
is to create and manage culture." But whether culture can be
altered by the intentional interventions of a leader is open to
question since, as Schein points out, it is more likely that culture controls leaders than that leaders control culture. If this
is accurate, it would not mean that leaders have no impact, but
rather that to be effective they must align their strategies with
their institution's culture rather than compete with it (Chaffee
and Tierney, 1988). Since institutions differ in their cultures,
actions that are effective on one campus setting may not be so
in another. It would follow that there may be few substantive
rules of leadership with general applicability. And it would also
be true that if leaders wish to influence their institution's culture they must first carefully study and understand it.

　　　To look at leadership through a cultural lens is not to im-
ply that rationality plays no part in organizational life. But it
does suggest that leaders may exert influence less through planning, decision making, and related administrative activities than
through affecting others' interpretations of institutional life. An
interpretive view of leadership emphasizes the importance of
leaders in developing and sustaining systems of belief that regenerate participants' commitment. Leaders accomplish this
through the use of language, symbolism, and ritual that cause
others to interpret organizational actions in ways consistent with
the values of the leader (Pfeffer, 1981). In this fashion, leaders
symbolically protect us from the uncertainties of an ambiguous
environment. As Bolman and Deal (1991, p. 404) put it, "They
help us feel less fearful and more confident. They help us find
attractive and plausible versions of what to think, feel, and do.
They help us see possibilities and discover resources."

　　　Since the interpretive way of viewing leadership has an
important place in this book, it is useful to think further about

how leadership and our interpretation or perception of reality are related.

Defining Reality

Reality is elusive. Consider *Tamara,* a play that was given in the Seventh Regiment Armory in New York City. There is no stage. The cast of ten characters moves continually throughout many rooms on the three floors of the Armory, so that two or more scenes may be played out simultaneously in different places in the building. If you were one of the 160 people in the audience for a performance, you could decide to stay in a single room for the entire play while characters came and went. Or you could choose to follow any character around from room to room for as long or short a time as you liked, or switch to another character whenever you wished. It is a most unusual way to experience theater, and the consequence, even though it is obvious, is startling. Since the choices you make determine the play you see, *everyone sees a different play.*

The question for the audience in *Tamara* is, How do you know what is important, when? Is a key episode taking place upstairs in the bedroom while you are downstairs watching a scene in the kitchen? Should you follow the butler or the heroine? Will an event that seems important at the moment have any bearing on the outcome, or will the drama hinge on some matter so apparently inconsequential at the time that no one paid it much attention? Suppose you didn't happen to observe that critical event, what then? And so it is that those who attend to one combination of events may believe they are watching a comedy of manners; those following another, a mystery; others, a melodrama. Which of these, or the many other partial interpretations of the complex reality at the Armory, provides the best sense of the whole?

In some ways, a college is like *Tamara.* It is a busy place, and those who take part in it have a limited amount of time. When they pay attention to one thing, they must reduce attention to another. It is very difficult to know if the things happening at the moment are important or not, and everyone has a somewhat different view of what is going on.

But a college is also different from *Tamara* in a critical way. If you watched the wrong actor in *Tamara* you could (in principle) later find out what was right by reading the script. But a college has no script. If there is any document that even resembles one, it is written after the action has taken place, not before, as people try to make sense out of what they have *already* seen and justify what they have *already* done.

Because it is so critical, I will belabor the obvious point: each individual who takes part in the life of a college will have a somewhat different sense of what is going on because he or she has followed different actors and witnessed different scenes. When college constituents engage in behavior others find bizarre, those others tend to blame it on the constituents' personalities; but if you really want to know *why* they do *what* they do — and to influence it — it is more useful to try to find out what part of the play they have been watching and what models they are using to try to figure out the nature of reality.

Moreover, colleges are exceptionally complex systems that interact with even more complex environments. They are made up of component parts, each of which is likely to engage in different internal activities and respond to different parts of the world outside itself. The people within these components fill different roles, have different experiences and expectations, and see different aspects of both the organization and the environment. No one in an organization can see all of it, much less understand all the ways in which its components are connected internally and externally.

However, despite our limited view, the things we see and the meanings we attach to them define our reality. We take those portions of the world we encounter and make sense of them by imposing on them patterns of meaning and attributions of cause and effect. Because we see only part of a complex environment and interpret what we see in a personal way, we often differ in our sense of what is real, what is important, what we should pay attention to, and what we should do about it. Objectively identical objects or incidents may have quite different meanings for different people.

Leadership and Reality

Given that individuals define reality differently, how is leadership related to their processes of locating reality? From a cultural and interpretive perspective, leadership principally involves a process by which "one or more individuals succeeds in attempting to frame and define the reality of others" (Smircich and Morgan, 1982, p. 258). Leadership means focusing the attention of others (Cyert, 1990) so that among the varied possible ways of separating figure and ground, they follow the one consistent with the leader's intentions. Leaders focus others' attention in order to "segment and point to portions of their experience and label it in consequential ways so that [others] take that segment more seriously and deal with it in a more organizationally appropriate manner" (Weick, 1990, p. 288). The function of leadership is to give the organizational audience a more pointed and consistent view of their scriptless *Tamara,* in which they are simultaneously participants and observers.

The leadership process involves social interactions that take place within a context in response to specific situations. It exists only in the relationship between "leader" and "led." It cannot be meaningfully studied without attending to this relationship. Indeed, since leadership is an interaction involving two or more people, the decision to single out a specific individual as the "leader" is often an arbitrary way of simplifying what is usually a complex and ultimately indeterminate web of cause and effect.

Leadership Action and Interpretation

Leadership involves something that an individual or a group *does.* This behavior may include an action that someone takes, such as attending (or not attending) a meeting, walking around the campus, responding to a question, or making a formal proposal. It may involve one person writing a document, raising an eyebrow, or returning a telephone call, or a group voting on a motion or debating a new program.

But actions do not speak for themselves. As we have just seen, they must be interpreted, and what may be seen by one observer as a clear act of leadership may be viewed differently by another. For example, actions which seem to one person to reflect creative and altruistic leadership may seem to another destructive and self-serving. At one college studied by the ILP, the president's unpopular decision to cut the personnel budget to meet an impending fiscal crisis was considered courageous leadership by trustees and traitorous capitulation by the faculty. And the union leader who called for a strike faced similar differences in the responses of various campus groups. Here are some of the factors that affect the way actions with leadership potential are interpreted.

Legitimation. Leadership involves behavior that is meant to influence others, but not all attempts at influence can be thought of as resulting in leadership. Behavior that is seen as coercive or manipulative, for example, may not only fail to influence now but may reduce the ability to influence in the future. Effective leadership involves behavior that others find appropriate given the circumstances and the nature of the relationship between the parties. The legitimacy of leadership behavior is always at bottom a matter of interpretation, and depends as much on the perceptions of the intended targets of influence as on the source. An individual's formal designation as president can contribute greatly to this interpretation of legitimacy, but cannot guarantee it.

Intentions. To be seen as a consequence of leadership, an outcome must be interpreted as reflecting, at least in part, the desires of the leader. An outcome may not affect perceptions of leadership if it is not seen as related to the leader's intentions or actions. However, because of the processes of social attribution (which relate outcomes to human agency rather than to external forces or to chance), and the tendency to search for causes to explain otherwise confusing events, people may perceive connections between outcomes and leaders' intentions where none exist. Since people in leadership roles are *expected* to cause events, others are more likely to focus attention on them and connect institutional events to them. Leaders, in turn, may promote such perceptions and attributions by seeking to take credit for the good outcomes and to absolve themselves of blame for the bad (a phenomenon memorialized in the phrase "the Teflon Presidency").

Initiative. Much of what happens in organizations occurs as people respond to normal and expected situations by following established formal or informal rules and norms. Behavior of this kind is not ordinarily thought of as involving leadership. Leadership is not routine; it requires an interpretation that a person has initiated a response to an expected situation in an unexpected way, or to an unexpected situation with the exercise of independent judgment and discretion. Often, the initiative will mean communication with another to begin an overt or tacit exchange of valued things (Burns, 1978). In such situations, effective leadership is ascribed when a leader's actions are seen as having positive consequences. As with legitimacy and intention, the extent to which a leader's behaviors are seen by others as not accounted for by rules is a matter of perception rather than fact; actions that can be interpreted as creative or novel by some may be seen by others as routine.

Morality. Because leaders are involved in interpreting nonroutine events and selecting one course of action over another, they are constantly called on to make value choices. These choices define the moral dimension of leadership, since they require leaders to act outside the guidance of rules as they articulate what they think an institution *should* be. When leaders do this, they are engaged in "conscious reflective intentional action" (Hodgkinson, 1991, p. 111). Aristotle called this "praxis," which is "ethical action in a political context, or purposeful human conduct, or behavior informed and guided by purposes, intentions, motives, morals, emotions, and values *as well as* the facts or 'science' of the case" (Hodgkinson, 1991, p. 43). To say that leadership has a moral quality is to say only that leaders' actions are based on ethical considerations, and not necessarily that the institution or its members have become more moral.

Behavior. Leadership initially changes perceptions, but it also eventually evokes changes in behavior. Such changes may occur in response to directive communications or—even in the absence of these communications—in anticipation of what the leader would wish to happen. Leadership can lead others to do different things, or to do things differently.

Although leadership must always be seen as eventually affecting the behavior of others, having this influence will depend on changed perceptions of reality and need not depend on changes in the objective environment. Since it is perception that defines reality, it is perception that must change. Leadership involves moving others toward a shared perception of reality, toward a common understanding of where the organization is and where it should be going, and toward an increased commitment to those ends.

Leaders and Leadership Roles

We normally think of leadership as directed downward in an organization, so that presidents influence vice presidents, deans influence faculty, and office directors influence secretaries. But a cultural and interpretive view of leadership emphasizes interaction and mutual influence and recognizes that a vice president can induce a president to act, a faculty member can cause a dean to interpret a situation from a different perspective, and a secretary can lead a director to select a different solution to a problem. In this way, "subordinates" also exhibit leadership, and it becomes clear that, by influencing in some way what others see or do, *everyone* in a college can, at least potentially, exhibit leadership at some time and under some circumstances. Distinguishing leaders from nonleaders is therefore less an analysis of what people do that influences others and affects outcomes than it is of the frequency with which they do (or are seen to do) these things and the breadth and significance of the issues that they affect.

Leadership is ubiquitous in human groups and emerges whenever two or more people engage in a collective activity (Hollander, 1985). As people interact over time, some are accorded higher status and more influence than others. In general, people achieve this level of status and influence because they are believed by others to represent to an unusual degree the values and skills considered important by the group. Group members with high status are more likely than those with lower status to initiate group activities and interaction, and their views and opinions are given greater weight than those of other group members.

Sometimes those identified as campus leaders have no formal position in the institutional hierarchy, but more frequently they do. When groups are informal, the emergence of leadership depends on the values of the group and the personalities and characteristics of its individual members. But when groups are formally structured, rationalized processes develop which create formal leadership roles. In higher education, selection of leaders by persons having the legal authority to do so (for example, the appointment of a trustee by a state governor), by direct constituent preference (for example, the election of a faculty senate chair by the faculty), and by representative groups (for example, selection of a dean by a faculty search committee) are all ways in which, depending on circumstances, leadership may be legitimately conferred on those filling leadership roles.

When the processes of selection are accepted by the members of the group, role incumbents are provided with a level of legitimacy that certifies and reinforces their higher status. Although college and university leaders may arise informally because of their personalities and skills, the ILP focused on persons who occupied leadership roles because they had been selected through formalized processes.

Presidents, senate chairs, trustees, faculty union presidents, deans, and many others fill formal leadership roles. A role is a set of expectations that people have about what the incumbent of a position is supposed to do. In a college, a leadership role is a formal campus position in which the incumbent is expected to exhibit leadership. Since people's expectations often overwhelm the information with which they are presented, those in leadership roles are often believed to exhibit leadership even when there is little objective evidence to support it.

These ideas about leadership, leaders, and leadership roles emphasize perceptions and interactions. They do not offer recipes for effective behavior. Presidents are considered effective leaders to the extent that they are seen to exhibit leadership and do what others consider good presidents should do. Similarly, good faculty senate leaders, good union leaders, good department leaders, or good board leaders are defined by the expectations and responses of followers. Because leadership is a process of interaction, it cannot be discussed or analyzed in any meaningful way without reference to those who are responsive to it. And since the expectations of followers are influenced by culture and interpretation, and may differ from campus to campus and situation to situation, there can be few substantive rules of good leadership.

These ideas suggest that the concepts of leadership, leader, and leadership role, although related, are not identical. People in leadership roles may not always be leaders or exhibit leadership. Those who exhibit leadership may not always be leaders or fill leadership roles. Because it is essential to make these distinctions, planning a study of leadership is as much a process of constructing a definition as it is of research design.

The Institutional Leadership Project

Everyone has a notion of the meaning of leadership in general, but neither its definition nor its measurement enjoys universal agreement. We may shrug off the problem of definition, and in the absence of accepted criteria suggest that we know leadership when we see it. But if we all see different things, then dialogue about leadership is problematic, preparing people for it is difficult, and understanding its consequences is impossible. The concept of leadership in organizations is particularly complex because certain people are expected to exhibit it by virtue of their positions and are subject to often severe criticism if they don't. Yet it is by no means clear what the "it" they are to exhibit is, and how it is related to organizational life or institutional change.

Since there is no agreement on what leadership is, there can be no agreement on how to study it. To study leadership is often to invent as much as to discover, and interpreting the findings perhaps as much an art as a science. So it is important to understand how the ILP went about the study of leadership, because the conclusions in this book cannot be judged independently of the definitions and understandings we began with, nor of the structure of the research that led to those conclusions.

The Institutional Leadership Project (ILP) was a five-year longitudinal study of formal leaders in thirty-two colleges and universities. The primary sources of information were interviews conducted at each of these institutions during the 1986–87 academic year, and again, in a follow-up visit, two years later in the 1988–89 academic year. With several exceptions, both sets of visits involved three days of on-site interviews conducted by one of four researchers using common and collaboratively developed sets of open-ended questions. A copy of the interview protocol used to interview "old presidents" during the initial campus visit is shown in Resource B. Slightly different protocols, but with many questions in common, were used to interview other categories of formal campus leaders.

The sessions were one to three hours in length, and those interviewed included the college president and other senior administrative officers, the chairs and heads of major committees of the board of trustees, and faculty leaders such as the present or former chair of the senate or comparable body, the head of the faculty union where one existed, and the chairs of important faculty committees. To protect confidentiality, all institutions in the study are henceforth referred to as "colleges," and all chief executive officers are called "presidents." Other institutional officers or organizational bodies are identified generically (for example, academic vice president, faculty senate, or faculty union), regardless of their actual titles. In total, 404 people were interviewed during visits in 1986–87, and 358 in 1988–89. Most organizations have informal as well as formal leaders, and indeed a good number of such individuals were identified in the course of the interviews. However, available resources limited the scope of research, and we could speak with only a few of them.

During the first round of interviews people were asked about how they worked together, communicated with each other, and reached judgments about institutional life. They were asked about campus goals, and how the behavior of leaders appeared to affect the achievement of those goals. And they were asked about how they learned and changed. Their responses provoked a number of ideas about how leaders act and think, some of them never before applied to higher education. These ideas included depictions of the processes through which new presidents learned and acted as they first "took charge" of their institutions, examinations of the different ways presidents and others thought about leadership, and considerations of the ways in which the cognitive "frames" and implicit leadership theories leaders used gave meaning to what they saw and affected their actions and the responses of others. The ILP also included studies of leader strategies, and of how these strategies changed as leaders became more experienced. Frames and strategies, in turn, led to explorations of "cognitive complexity" and the extent to which differences in the ability to see problems through multiple perspectives affected how leaders acted. The most salient of these and other ideas, and the data supporting them, will be summarized throughout the book. More extensive analyses of the concepts, the methodologies used to study them, and the relevant data are contained in the ILP research studies listed in Resource D and Resource C.

Several of these ideas and findings were used to develop the interview protocols for the follow-up visits in 1988–89, but in addition, particular attention was given to asking how the campus had changed during the two years between visits, to see if various aspects of leadership were associated with organizational change.

Institutions were purposively selected so that the study would include the largest and most representative sectors of American higher education and reflect their diversity (see Birnbaum, Bensimon, and Neumann, 1989, for a description of the sampling procedure). The thirty-two institutions included eight from each of four categories — universities, four-year state colleges, four-year independent colleges, and two-year community colleges. A list of participating institutions is shown in Resource A.

In order to ensure diversity, institutions from within each category were selected for the sample based on differences in Carnegie classification, governance sponsorship, educational program, unionization, or institutional system membership. Other factors, such as national geographic distribution of all institutions, enrollment size, and urban or rural location were also considered. Particular attention was given to the representation of female and minority presidents in the sample.

When studying a complex and ambiguous phenomenon such as organizational leadership, every potential research design involves making trade-offs. In this study, the trade-off of greatest significance is that studying a small number of institutions in moderate depth meant forgoing both the richness of understanding that might have been provided by an intensive ethnographic study of a single institution and the breadth that might have been afforded by gathering survey data from a large number of institutions.

Less evident were the analytical consequences of selecting a purposive sample to discover patterns that appeared consistent across institutions with different characteristics. The conscious decision that institutions should not be selected randomly meant that statistical tests could not be used to generalize the findings to higher education as a whole. As a result, the validity of the findings should not be assessed by statistical significance, but by verisimilitude. Signs that the findings reported here are more generally applicable will emerge from the extent to which readers see their own institutions reflected in these pages, or find that the results help them to make better sense of patterns and relationships with which they are already familiar.

How This Study Is Different

A visit to the business section of any good bookstore will convince you that the study of leadership, long ignored, has recently become something of a cottage industry. There has been a renaissance in studying leadership in higher education as well. What is the justification for yet more research? In part, the answer can be found in the differences in methods, samples, and research approaches. Other studies have tended either to look at institutions and presidents at one moment in time, examine one institutional type, focus almost exclusively on the president, study only "effective" presidents, or rely on single sources of data. In contrast, the ILP was longitudinal, contained many institutional types, considered multiple leadership roles, included obscure as well as renowned institutions, and used a number of different sources of data. The ILP also differed from other works in several important ways that have particular relevance for higher education.

Culture and Interpretation

Studies of academic leadership have tended to focus on institutions as rational, goal-seeking organizations that emphasize the importance of leaders' characteristics and actions and prescribe what leaders should do to be effective. In contrast, the ILP viewed institutions as cultural systems in which leaders and others construct social reality through the interpretations they make of equivocal events.

Presidential Term

Relatively few studies of leadership have specifically emphasized the difference between leaders who are relatively new to their roles and those who have been in their positions for a longer period. It is intuitively apparent that newly appointed leaders might well have to spend their time differently than those who have become familiar with an institution's culture and with the intricacies of their office. It might also be expected that leaders should change in other ways as they gain more experience in office. ILP institutions were selected so that the sample contained equal numbers of new presidents (in office for three years or less) and old presidents (in office for five years or more), matched for institutional type and other organizational characteristics.

How Leaders Think

Most previous research on college and university leadership has emphasized who leaders are and what they do. While the ILP devoted some attention to these questions, the emphasis on the interpretive roles of leaders led to an examination of the ways leaders think and learn. In particular, we gave attention to the cognitive frames or "lenses" through which leaders see their organizations, the ways in which they think about the strategic actions they should take, and the implicit models of leadership that influence how they enact their roles.

A Note on Leadership Research

The research design of the ILP was ambitious in order to try to improve comprehension and integration in a research field characterized by fragmentation and confusion. Chaffee (1989a) has called for leadership research in higher education that explicitly defines the researcher's perspectives, uses multiple points of view, and avoids narrow focus. Yukl (1981, p. 287) has similarly argued for studies "with a perspective broad enough to encompass leader traits, behavior, influence processes, intervening variables, situational variables, and end-result variables." *How Academic Leadership Works* is offered as one response to these calls for a more holistic approach to the study of institutional leadership.

CHAPTER 2

Myths and Mysteries of Academic Leadership

Most of us approach discussions of leadership with some common preconceptions about it firmly in mind. Since we see what we expect to see, these preconceptions may act as filters that influence how we perceive and interpret new information. It will be useful, before discussing the results of the ILP in detail, to specifically confront some fundamental ideas about leadership that might otherwise obscure or bias an understanding of the material that will be presented later.

In this chapter I use some findings of the ILP to refute five familiar myths about academic leadership and to discuss three mysteries whose solutions may change the way we think of leadership in the future.

Myths of Academic Leadership

Although leadership is generally considered to be important, it is a vague and in many ways undefinable process. Humans, seeking understanding in the midst of ambiguity, develop shared meanings to resolve uncertainty, make actions seem reasonable, and create satisfying explanations of causes (Kuh and Whitt, 1988). The constant repetition of these shared meanings makes them appear real, in spite of (or perhaps because of) the lack of evidence to support them. Such beliefs can be referred to as myths.

A myth, as I use the term, is a widely believed social construction of reality that has not been — and perhaps cannot be — empirically verified (Scott, 1981). A myth is not necessarily false, and in fact most myths contain at least some element of truth. But myths can be misleading, because they suggest oversimplified ways of interpreting exceptionally complex phenomena. And they can misdirect; a leader who acts on the basis of a myth can make major errors of judgment.

The Myth of Presidential Vision

If there is one thing on which almost all those who write about leadership agree, it is that successful leaders must have a vision and be able to communicate it to others. The words used may be somewhat different, but, "no matter what it is called — personal agenda, purpose, legacy, dream, goal, or vision — the intent is the same. Leaders must be forward-looking and have a clear sense of the direction that they want their organization to take" (Kouzes and Posner, 1987, p. 85).

The myth is not that a vision —"a view of a realistic, credible, attractive future" (Bennis and Nanus, 1985, p. 89) — is important to have, but that the vision must be developed by presidents as the outgrowth of their own personal agendas. The mark of effective leadership according to the myth, therefore, becomes getting others to "buy in" to the leader's vision. But seen from an interpretive perspective, the real purposes of articulating a vision are to give constituents confidence in the leader's competence and convince them that the leader has listened to them and been influenced by them. These two outcomes then make it possible for a leader to subtly influence constituents' perceptions of reality and move them toward shared views of desirable futures. Leaders do this, not through rational argument or political power, but by changing constituents' perceptions of figure and ground and focusing their attention on certain elements already existing in the organization rather than others. These two outcomes are thus also the mark of a good leader, since the interpretive view defines success and effectiveness in leadership in terms of levels of constituent support. (This definition will be discussed in detail in Chapter Three.)

Constituents want to have confidence that their leaders know where they are going. The sense of direction is not important as much for its content — within limits — as for its symbolic value. The articulation of a vision is a means through which faculty develop confidence in a president's ability to make sense of ambiguity and appropriately manage the institution. It is through this articulation that leaders "provide members of the organization with a sense that they are organized, even amidst an everyday feeling that at a detailed level everything runs the danger of falling apart" (Smircich and Morgan, 1982, p. 260).

Leaders engender confidence through presenting a vision, but the vision is not something created out of whole cloth. The vision must be an articulation of the college-that-might-be that reflects the interests — manifest or latent — of constituents. An acceptable vision does not say, "Here is where *I* want us to be," but rather, "Here is where you have told me *you* really want to go." The leader's vision is more a symbol of having listened to and respected the visions of others than an expression of the leader's goals. To present a vision that is accepted as legitimate, leaders should follow the advice given by one of the ILP presidents to "do a lot of listening. And when you do that, solicit the dreams and hopes from the people. Tell the people the good things you are finding. And in three to six months, take these things and report them as the things you would like to see happen."

A shared vision tells constituents, not necessarily that the institution will be different, but that it will be better. A vision that creates a common sense of reality selects from among an institution's existing goals those to which special prominence should be given. The leader, through an understanding of the institution's culture, is able to present this new emphasis as consistent with core institutional values and traditions. Once articulated, the vision provides a sense-making lens through which the leader's substantive ideas can be assessed and understood. It sets up the framework that allows others to connect what is being proposed to the shared values of the institution. An action that may be rejected by constituents as arbitrary or capricious without an articulated vision may be embraced with one.

Consider how three ILP presidents failed to create a shared vision because they tried to create a presidential vision. One president, asked by members of a beleaguered faculty to give the presidential vision in the next state-of-the-college address, spoke of the college as an exemplar of cultural and ethnic diversity. The speech was considered a disappointment, because faculty had wanted to hear about their vision of innovation and experimentation in teaching.

A faculty leader at another campus told how the president transmitted goals to the faculty: "He gives them to us each year at the first faculty meeting. He just drones on and on. Every year, he has a list of goals and then he reads it to us. It is *dismal*. Would you like to have goals handed down to you?" The president of a third campus wrote a college academic plan shortly after taking office. Faculty complained because they saw it as a document developed unilaterally, without faculty input. The president's evident disregard for process and focus on task caused the faculty to deny ownership of the plan and the vision behind it.

In contrast, a president who successfully changed campus interpretations of a desirable future described how she went about the process of developing a vision: "When I arrived the media wanted to know what my plans were for the college, what changes I would be making. But I never thought of the presidency in those terms. What I spent a lot of time on was letting people know that I would not be imposing my version of the truth. Together we shaped a vision of the college. We have not moved in radically new directions. We are expanding and redefining the mission in some ways."

Similarly, Neumann analyzed how a successful ILP president — that is, one with high constituent support — metaphorically "infected people with vision." The president articulated a vision that was developed after extensive discussions with important campus constituents. He listened carefully and respected what he heard. He connected the vision to the college's history and values, and grounded it in the college as it presently existed. In contrast to the three failures of vision mentioned earlier, this president's statement was seen as "fundamentally authentic to [the college] —

an unearthing and synthesis of the college's central beliefs — it was, in fact, highly catching" (Neumann, 1991a, p. 9).

The myth of presidential vision is that leaders must set the direction for the college and move people toward achieving those goals. The reality of presidential vision is that goals are already within the institution, waiting to be both discovered and renewed through interpretation. As one president said, "I think that a president who announces what the vision of an institution is on day one is asking for trouble. You need to alter the vision to be consistent with the culture, or you have to let it emerge from what is being talked about on campus." The most effective visions turn out to be those that embody the perspectives of constituents in idealized form (Conger and Kanungo, 1988).

The Myth of the President as Transformational Leader

Some higher education analysts believe that too many college and university presidents passively respond to internal and external pressures. These analysts propose that many of the problems of higher education could be corrected if only presidents would act to transform their institutions.

Beginning with the work of Burns (1978), scholars have attempted to differentiate between two forms of leadership, transactional and transformational. In concept, transactional leadership understands and conforms to the culture of an organization as it exists. It emphasizes means, and attempts to meet the needs of followers. Transactional leadership depends on the exchange of desired goods between leader and follower, and the relationship continues as long as the exchange is considered satisfactory by both.

Transformational leadership, on the other hand, emphasizes values and goals such as liberty, justice, and equality and emphasizes motivating followers to support leader-intended change. Transformational leadership introduces and advances new cultural forms. It fosters the creation of a more enduring bond between leader and follower as they move each other toward higher levels of motivation and morality.

Because our society gives such emphasis to the importance of leadership, the concept of transformational leadership is particularly seductive. One slogan suggests that transactional leaders are merely managers who do things right, while transformational leaders inspire followers to do the right things. Given a choice, most leaders would probably prefer to put their energies into engaging the hearts and minds of others than into confronting budgets, legislators, and unions and managing through transactional means the other everyday problems of running a complex organizational system. But how realistic is such a preference?

The duality of transaction and transformation, which appeared to bring new clarity to discussions of leadership, turned out to be a distinction without any real meaning for colleges and universities (Bensimon, in press; Bensimon, Neumann, and Birnbaum, 1989). Transformational leadership, through which extraordinary people change organizational goals and values, is an anomaly in higher education. Because the goals and enduring purposes of an academic institution are likely to be shaped by its history, its culture, and the socialization and training of its participants, rather than by an omnipotent leader, attempts at transformational leadership are more likely to lead to disruption and conflict than to desirable outcomes.

Purely transactional leadership in higher education, content with the status quo and interested only in management, is only slightly less rare than purely transformational leadership. While present on some campuses, it is far more the exception than the rule. Most presidents are conservative; they do not want to revolutionize a system in which they have been exceptionally successful. But at the same time they are seldom content to be figureheads. Presidents have strong egos and high achievement motivation. They understand that the president's role involves not just helping the institution run smoothly but making institutional progress at the same time.

Good presidents among the ILP institutions could not be characterized as either purely transactional or transformational but were seen to synthesize the two approaches. Transactional leaders may emphasize *supporting* the status quo, and transformational leaders may focus on *changing* the organization in a revolutionary way; in contrast, good presidents in the ILP emphasized restoring values and *improving* behavior in an evolutionary way. They did not consider values more important than instrumental activities, but realized that if they were to have influence they must attend to both.

For example, almost all respondents at one ILP campus identified the new president as responsible for major positive changes in institutional quality, morale, reputation, and financial condition. They pointed to his willingness to make decisions, to take risks, to change senior personnel, to restructure the college, and to balance the budget as key elements in his success. Many referred to him as a transformational leader. But a closer examination indicated how his success depended on a careful reading of institutional circumstances. Constituents believed that institutional survival was in jeopardy, and they saw supporting the new president as a last hope. One faculty leader said, "He benefited from the fear here that the institution was declining. Our success fell on the shoulders of the president. There was a clear feeling that we were going to make it or not make it with this man." Another faculty leader acknowledged, "He did not make major changes in the heart of the college. When he came here everyone was suffering. Everyone saw programs being weakened because there had been no priorities. He said to us, 'It is up to you folks; we can cut or keep on drifting along.' No one was against change."

Academic institutions are often accused of hypocrisy, of claiming they possess virtues or engage in activities that they do not. Cohen and March (1974) suggest that institutions should not treat this kind of hypocrisy as a moral failure but as evidence of a desire for a transition between what the institution actually is and what it claims to be and, in fact, wants to be. Good leaders help change their institutions, not through transformation and the articulation of new goals or values, but through transactions that emphasize selected values already in place and move the institution toward attaining them. Good leaders reduce organizational hypocrisy.

One exposition of this view has been presented by Bensimon, Neumann, and Birnbaum (1989, p. 75):

It would appear that it is good transactional leadership that affects the life of most colleges most of the
time. . . . The rarity of successful transformational
leadership makes it all the more noticeable when
it is manifest. But because it is so often related to
a complex web of situational contingencies, idiosyncratic personalities, and chance events, little
likelihood exists that its nature can ever be truly
understood or its frequency increased. This situation is not necessarily a cause for despair, however;
organizations can probably tolerate only a limited
level of transformation, and the constant changes
of values induced by a succession of transformational leaders would severely threaten both the stability of institutions and the systems of mutual interaction of which they are a part.

Those who espouse the importance of transformational leadership should pause to consider what life would be like in an organization whose programs, procedures, and core values could
be called into question by each new president.

The Myth of Presidential Charisma

Webster's Ninth New Collegiate Dictionary defines charisma as a "personal magic of leadership arousing special popular loyalty or
enthusiasm." The word *magic* is appropriate, because charisma
implies a compelling but mysterious ability to lead that is difficult
to define or understand. Charismatic leadership gives little attention to structure, routine, and established order, and relies
instead on the magnetic personal qualities of the leader. It pre-
sumes that people want leaders they can revere, or even idol-
ize, and that such leaders are able to motivate followers to support the leader's goals in preference to their own.

Several of the ILP presidents who were well thought of
by their boards, faculties, and administrative colleagues were
described as charismatic. One of these was characterized as having "the persona one would identify with a college president.

He has charisma, presence, image, reputation. If you are in a room with him, you sense his presence. It's commitment, intensity, how he views the institution and speaks about it." However, since charisma was an attribution made by others, there was not universal agreement on whether it existed in each instance — what one person saw as charisma another could see as willful egoism. Nor was it independent of context. Based on the few cases in which ILP presidents had previously served as a chief executive officer, or had left an ILP institution during the course of the study to serve as president elsewhere, presidents seen as charismatic in their present positions may not have been so seen in their previous institutions and may not be so judged in the next. Nevertheless, the perceived possession of charisma could have an enormous effect on the willingness of others to believe in and support programs and ideas associated with the leader. A faculty member told how a former president came into the institution with immediate faculty support because of his previous institutional association, national reputation, and the fact that "he delegated, he listened, he provided moral inspiration." This president endorsed without faculty protest a project for which his predecessor had failed to get faculty approval, "an indication of his charisma and moral authority."

But if several successful ILP presidents were described as charismatic, so too were several presidents who had lost campus support and were perceived as unsuccessful. Charisma can be a two-edged sword. It provides some leaders with an extra measure of influence that moves their institutions toward higher levels of performance (Bass, 1985). It also has a dark side. Charismatics sometimes have an unhealthy narcissism that can lead to a grandiose sense of certainty, disdain for subordinates, unwillingness to tolerate dissent, and a sense that normal rules don't apply to them (Goleman, 1990). Reliance on personal charisma can diminish the authority of others in the hierarchy, weaken the formal administrative structure of an institution, and leave a college in shambles if the leader suddenly fails or leaves. Charisma can reduce interaction, and lead to acceptance of a leader's acts on faith rather than understanding.

An example of the problematic side of charisma was seen on a troubled ILP campus at which a faculty leader described the president as "very charismatic, and perhaps relies too much on that." This president believed that it was important to become "totally independent of people. You must have enough confidence in yourself to sift through what people say; the hidden agendas are many, and you have to make your own decisions." This distancing from constituents increased the attribution of personal charisma, but also isolated the president and distorted the administrative infrastructure. When she made a unilateral decision that angered the faculty, there were no backup systems to maintain institutional functioning during a time of campus crisis.

There were only a few examples among ILP colleges where charisma helped rather than hindered the institution, and it is likely that in higher education in general, charismatic leaders have created more problems than solutions. Moreover, although it has been claimed that "anyone of reasonable intelligence and high motivation can develop charismatic characteristics" (Fisher, 1984, p. 42), most scholars believe that no one knows the exact source of charisma, or how it can be cultivated. It is just as probable that perceived success leads others to attribute charisma to leaders as it is that charisma leads to perceived success, and that those who are seen as good leaders "are granted a certain degree of respect and even awe by their followers, which increases the bond of attraction between them" (Bennis and Nanus, 1985, p. 224). Calls for more charismatic leaders are thus likely to be of little value.

An attribution of charisma depends not only on the characteristics of the leader, but also on the implicit theories of leadership held by the follower (Bass, 1985). The qualities of charisma are general enough that they can be represented by many different behaviors, each of which is subject to interpretation by followers, based on factors such as the situation and the previous relationship with the leader (Avolio and Yammarino, 1990). Even those who believe in the importance of charismatic leadership warn that it usually is not found in old, highly structured, and successful organizations, but in old institutions that are in crisis or new ones trying to survive (Bass, 1985). Effective charismatic leadership may be rare in higher education because the training and socialization of faculty predisposes them to resist hierarchical authority of any kind, and because most colleges are functioning effectively.

The most critical problem with reliance on charisma is that it may cause a college to ignore the processes of institution-building — the development of norms of shared responsibility — which may leave it unable to function effectively when the charismatic leader leaves the scene. Charisma may be most constructive when it is used to develop an institution's infrastructure and increase the dispersal of leadership throughout the organization, and most disruptive when it leads an institution to be seen merely as the lengthened shadow of the leader.

Determining the real impact of a charismatic president is difficult. Even when charismatics fail as leaders and prove costly to their institutions, they may still project qualities commonly associated with good leadership because they have "considerable talent for self-presentation and the capacity to create favorable impressions" of themselves (Hogan, Raskin, and Fazzini, 1990, p. 352). The potential of charisma to substitute this kind of impression management for substance led one ILP president to comment that "charismatic leadership at best is an exaggeration and at worst it is mischievous because it makes presidents sound semireligious. Leadership is hard work; that is the other side of my skepticism about charismatic leadership. You cannot articulate a global vision and walk away. The real problem of leadership is translating [the vision] into practical things."

The Myth of Presidential Distance

It has been suggested (Fisher, 1984) that leaders in general, and college presidents in particular, can increase their power by remaining distant from their followers and that presidential effectiveness diminishes as they increase interaction with constituents. Belief in this myth might cause presidents to avoid situations leading to close personal relationships with colleagues,

Source: Copyright 1987 by Herblock in the *Washington Post.* Reprinted with permission.

and to maximize status differences, emphasize the trappings of office, and give too much attention to ceremonial functions.

The data collected by the ILP lend no credence to this myth. They suggest instead that faculty support of their president is more often related to comparative closeness than distance. In her analysis of the factors used by constituents to assess ILP presidents, for example, Fujita (1990) found that presidents seen as reaching out to faculty—soliciting their opinions, dropping into their offices, eating lunch with them—were more highly supported than those seen as insular, unapproachable, or authoritarian.

This is not to deny that presidents who are seen to be effective have higher status than most of their constituents, and that this difference in status may strengthen their influence. But if status differences get too large, communication may be reduced. This may lead campus associates to feel that they can no longer influence the president, thus diminishing presidential power. To the extent that the relations between presidents and constituents can be located on a continuum with polar values of familiarity and distance, the most effective position is somewhere in between the two poles.

Because presidential distance is already created and reinforced by the typical hierarchical structure of a college administration and status differences are inherent in the leadership role, presidents seldom need to act to create distance. Instead, if they are to achieve the proper balance, they should give more attention to reducing distance.

The findings of the ILP indicate that efforts of presidents to replace distance with engagement were usually recognized and could end up strengthening a president's influence. One faculty leader described how a new president went about diminishing status differences by rejecting formal protocol and visiting with faculty where they worked: "I remember exactly the moment when I realized what kind of president he would be. I was at a planning meeting, we were just sitting around the table and suddenly I noticed him. He had just come in and not done anything to call attention to himself. You could see he wasn't burdened with a sense of his own importance. And then he said a couple of things in a way that made us want to go out and do them."

The effect of presidential distance or engagement cannot be specified in advance, because it is contingent on an institution's specific culture. As in most social situations that are interpreted through reciprocal transactions, the most effective behaviors of a leader are those that fulfill the expectations of constituents. Leaders who violate these cultural expectations, either by being seen as too distant or too familiar, are likely to find their effectiveness diminished.

The Myth of Presidential Style and Traits

Early traditions of leadership research assumed causal relationships between leadership styles and organizational outcomes.

It was believed that once these relationships were determined, it would be possible either to select leaders who already possessed these successful styles or to train leaders who didn't possess them to use them in order to achieve desired objectives. Unfortunately, the idea of style has increasingly emphasized superficial aspects of behavior and has lost sight of the "deep structure" of leadership, which includes "elusive concepts that have no physical, behavioral counterpart" (Pondy, 1978, p. 89).

Neither the ILP, nor most other analyses of leaders in academic or nonacademic settings, have identified any successful one-style-fits-all approach to leadership. Traits described as essential by one study are found to be of little importance by another. Effective and ineffective academic leaders come in all sizes, shapes, colors, genders, levels of experience, and personalities. They are almost all intelligent and articulate because they work in academic environments that give extraordinary value to these characteristics, but the most intelligent or smooth-tongued are not necessarily the most successful, nor are presidents likely to be either smarter or more articulate than all of their faculty constituents. Instead, the effectiveness of different styles appears to depend on subordinates' expectations, environmental contingencies, and values and perceptions related to organizational culture (Smith and Peterson, 1988).

The ILP data are in accord. They too suggest that leadership must be considered in context; the ideas that some presidents can be successful in any setting, that there are characteristics that can serve to screen potential presidential applicants in a candidate pool, or that embracing certain traits such as aloofness can increase the chances of success are surely misleading and potentially dangerous.

Only consummate actors can be successful and believable when they attempt to be what they are not and act contrary to their own instincts and values. The ILP data show that to the extent any characteristics or traits differentiate between successful and unsuccessful leaders, they involve perceptions by constituents that presidents are willing to be influenced, that they are competent, and that they respect the institution's traditions (Fujita, 1990). A word frequently used by constituents to describe successful presidents is "integrity." Constituents can develop these perceptions only when their presidents act authentically and are seen by others as credible and trustworthy.

Mysteries of Academic Leadership

Although writing on leadership is abundant, surprisingly little research attention has been given to three mysteries whose solutions may have important consequences for higher education. Is academic leadership improved through the use of teams? Does the experience with which presidents assume their positions affect their performance? Do men and women behave differently as presidents, or have different effects on their colleges? When people assume that the answers to these questions are self-evident, the answers may acquire the status of myths and have the same pernicious effects on perception and behavior as the myths that concern presidential vision, transformational leadership, charisma, distance, and style.

The ILP was not designed specifically to respond to these questions. However, some data bearing on them, collected during the course of campus visits, provide provocative clues. Analyses by several ILP researchers suggest that while the final answers are still unknown, the questions provide interesting directions for future inquiry.

The Mystery of Leadership and Teams

Does effective leadership in higher education require the development of good administrative teams (Green, 1988b; Gardiner, 1988), or can presidents achieve comparable results without involving senior colleagues as relative equals in regular, collective, face-to-face interaction? The organizational literature disagrees on whether institutional productivity is enhanced by teamwork or by individual entrepreneurship. However, the prevalent belief, based on findings in business organizations, suggests that "organizational success, regardless of whether it is defined as the ability to innovate, achieve adaptability in adverse circumstances, or get an edge on productivity, is more likely to be achieved when leaders embrace a teamwork approach" (Bensimon, 1991a, p. 19).

Although there is little research based on academic institutions, this view of the value of teams is clearly consistent with academic norms of collegiality and shared governance. But do teams really make a difference? The ILP examined administrative teams from several different perspectives.

President and Vice President Teams. Lathrop (1990) studied the smallest form of team, consisting of only two people, in her analysis of working relationships between presidents and their academic vice presidents (AVP) in the thirty-one ILP institutions for which data were available. She used interview data to examine the frequency and formality of the interaction of presidents and academic vice presidents and the level of status differences between them. Two types of relationship were of particular interest.

Directive relationships were seen in about one-quarter of the colleges. The president assumed a position of authority over the AVP, and they spent little time together. Most communications were formal, and frequently in writing. The president attempted to maintain control over academic activities in the institution and advised, informed, and directed the AVP about decisions or actions that should be taken. In general, the relationship was unidirectional, with influence flowing from superior to subordinate.

Collaborative relationships existed in over half the institutions. The president and AVP worked side by side as colleagues. Communications were frequent and informal and could be initiated by either party. Both were involved in making major decisions, and each influenced the other. This kind of relationship most closely exhibited the characteristics commonly associated with a team.

When a panel of experienced administrators assessed the probable campus consequences of these different relationships, the results were dramatic. All collaborative pairs were assessed as reflecting good working relationships that were likely to provide effective campus leadership. All directive pairs were believed to have poor working relationships that were unlikely to provide effective leadership. The panel predicted that collaborative pairs would be more likely than directive pairs to share institutional goals and visions for the future and to identify each other as important campus leaders.

These predictions were not supported by the data. Moreover, the presence of collaboration was not related to faculty support of the president or to college change over two years. The attractive notion that the team relationship of a president and academic vice president has a significant effect on the patterns of college life or the outcomes of college situations thus remains unproven.

Administrative Teams. Presidents and AVPs form one kind of shared leadership in many institutions. But AVPs are not the only senior administrators with whom a president works, and other leadership groups in the form of cabinets or related bodies exist on almost all campuses. When such a group acts in a manner that develops collaborative leadership, it can be considered to be a team.

Bensimon (1991a) studied a subsample of thirteen ILP presidents to try to understand how these teams worked. All the presidents had a group of senior administrators with whom they routinely met. But while all presidents had administrative *groups,* not all presidents had administrative *teams.* Six of the thirteen presidents described their administrative groups as involved in both making decisions and determining the future direction of their campuses, and not used solely as a means of delivering information to and from the college population. The presidents made full and comprehensive use of these groups, and they could be thought of as real leadership teams. In addition to whatever influence they had in their individual positions, team members also affected campus outcomes through their collective behavior.

The other seven presidents had administrative groups that performed limited functions, usually with an emphasis on delivering information or progress reports. These groups also tended to emphasize the importance of loyalty to the president. They were identified as illusory teams, because — although they worked collectively — as team members, they were more likely to act as agents of the president than as participants in a joint enterprise of leadership.

How important are leadership teams? Although the small size of the group makes it difficult to say anything about these possible relationships with great confidence, there were no obvious relationships between the use of real or illusory teams and effectiveness as shown by constituent ratings of the president or measures of institutional change. Neumann's (1991c) analysis of ILP data indicates that administrators who participated in real teams were more satisfied with their roles and with the quality of their deliberations than those who did not. Administrative satisfaction is itself a desirable outcome that may justify greater attention to teams. But in terms of institutional performance, the effect of teams is still unclear. Working together may be important, but whether leadership, in order to be perceived as effective, requires regular face-to-face interaction in the context of a real team, or merely continual communication with "disassembled" teams of individuals or ad hoc groups that shift from issue to issue, is at present unknown.

The Mystery of Leadership and Experience

How much experience, and of what kind, is necessary for presidential leadership to be perceived as successful? In general, earlier experiences that might be expected to help turned out not to do so. For example, it might be anticipated that previous experience as a faculty member or a vice president for academic affairs would be important for a successful presidential term, but neither appeared related to constituent support or measures of institutional change. It is true that most presidents had significant experience in a higher education position; perhaps what counts is experience itself, rather than its particular kind.

Why might experience be important? Administrators make decisions in two kinds of ways — logical and nonlogical (Simon, 1987). Nonlogical decisions, based on what we commonly think of as "intuition," involve responses that must take place so quickly there is no time for a sequential analysis. Even in retrospect, an administrator, although certain of the decision, may be unable to articulate the reasons for it. Experts in many fields are able to make quick and accurate judgments because they have, over time and through experience, acquired a great deal of infor-

mation that falls into recognized patterns for them. Faced with
a new situation, such experts may not have to try to solve the
problem logically, or consciously, because they can rely on these
patterns derived from recollections of earlier situations.

Research studies of experts in many fields confirm the par-
ticulars. Those with experience are more likely than those with
less experience to perceive meaningful patterns and visualize
problems at more generalized levels. They give more attention
to qualitative analysis of a problem, attend more to simulta-
neous cues, and act more to separate the important from the
trivial (Glaser and Chi, 1988; Berliner, 1988). On the other
hand, experts may sometimes perform less effectively and make
less accurate judgments because their oversensitivity to subtle
cues in specific cases may lead them to overlook more mundane
types of information that is routinely available (Johnson, 1988).

Does having previous presidential experience make a
difference in what presidents do when they begin a new appointment? Bensimon (1987) found in one ILP study that experienced
presidents appeared to have learned a great deal from their previous positions and approached their new positions in different
ways than first-time presidents. They gave more attention to
learning aggressively and systematically about the new institution before their arrival, to mastering the budget, and to learning about college history and culture. They were less likely to
approach their institutions with preconceived plans of action and
more attentive to the subtleties of institutional life.

Several experienced ILP presidents explicitly commented
on the differences between their old and new institutions; others
were convinced that the approach they had found successful before could serve as well for their new positions. Previous experience, therefore, may either sensitize presidents to contingencies and enable them to make more accurate assessments of the
unique characteristics of new environments, or lead them toward
increased certainty that institutions are similar and their experiences can be generalized.

Learning from experience is not automatic; presidents can
learn only when they are able to notice errors and outcomes
that are contrary to expectations. The human bias to search for

confirming, rather than disconfirming, evidence may lead some presidents to systematically misinterpret what they hear from constituents (Feldman, 1986). Neumann's (1990) ILP study of presidents' perceptions of their own errors suggests that this is more likely to happen with experience; presidents were more likely to identify errors as occurring early rather than late in their presidential careers. One explanation for this might be that presidents make fewer mistakes as they gain experience. However, Neumann's analysis, which is consistent with data reported later in this book, suggests that it is more probable that some presidents may be less likely to receive or process negative feedback as they gain experience. Neumann also identified a group of ILP presidents who were unable to recall that they had *ever* made a major error. These presidents also seemed insensitive to the cultural and interpretive realities of their institutions; their limited ability to interpret social cues or detect errors diminished their ability to learn and change.

When experience leads presidents to listen to others and be responsive to their concerns, it may promote more effective learning and perceptions of more effective leadership in new organizational settings. But when it leads presidents to be more secure in their own judgments, to discount negative feedback, and to ignore the cultural differences that create different realities by producing multiple perceptions of each situation or event, experience may lead to less effective learning and consequently to failed leadership. The relationship of presidential success to experience—how much, of what kind, in what setting—is therefore not yet clearly understood.

The Mystery of Leadership and Gender

Do men and women think or behave differently as leaders? If so, do these differences have implications for their institutions? If leadership is an invented social construct, as this book asserts, and if gender differences are critical to the ways in which we experience and make sense of the social world, as many feminist theorists have argued, then there may be an important relationship between gender and leadership.

The ILP research described in this book found no apparent relationships between gender and leadership, either in terms of presidential background, the way presidents thought, constituent support, or institutional change. This lack of relationship is consistent with some other studies of leadership in academic settings. For example, in his review of administrative behavior in higher education, Dill (1984) found that the decision-making behavior of men and women was more similar than dissimilar, and Van der Veer (1991) found no difference between men and women in the cognitive complexity of mid- or upper-level academic executives.

However, studies of male and female corporate leaders present conflicting evidence about the importance of gender. Kanter (1977, p. 199), for example, argued that there is no research evidence that leadership aptitude or style is gender related, and suggested that such theories "do not match the realities of adult life in organizations." On the other hand, it has been proposed (Rosener, 1990, p. 120) not only that gender-related differences in leadership styles exist, but that women succeed "because of — not in spite of — certain characteristics generally considered to be 'feminine' and inappropriate in leaders." These "feminine" characteristics include encouraging participation, sharing power and information, and enhancing the self-worth of others. They are contrasted with the "traditional command-and-control style" (p. 120) said to be associated with male leaders. Similar arguments suggesting that women have particular strengths well suited to the newer approaches to effective leadership have been advanced for colleges as well (Shavlik and Touchton, 1988).

Feminist scholarship is also beginning to think about the question of leadership and gender in ways that suggest these are differences to be acknowledged. Bensimon (1989a), for example, compared the meaning of leadership as defined by two ILP presidents, one male and one female, and reported that their responses represented significantly different perspectives on leadership that were consistent with feminist theories. The male president's view of leadership was instrumental and separatist and focused on the organization's potential for change; the female president's view was expressive and integrated and focused on the leader's potential for change.

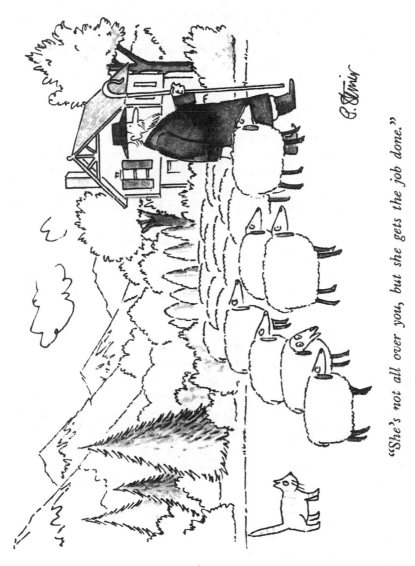

"She's not all over you, but she gets the job done."

It may be that there are important gender-related differences among leaders that were not made visible by the ILP because of our own preconceptions or the methods we used. What is also still to be discovered in this developing line of inquiry is whether these differences, if they truly exist, affect leader behavior or institutional outcomes.

While the subtleties of gender differences remain a matter for further research, the aggregate findings of the ILP make one thing clear; in terms of the major factors considered in this study, women are no less effective than men as presidents. Still, they are apparently *seen* differently. Some women presidents report, for example, that as candidates they had been patronized by trustee search committees, grilled more extensively on financial issues than male candidates would have been, and in other ways made to feel that while a man's competence may be assumed, a woman's competence is constantly questioned and must be proven (Leatherman, 1991; Vaughan, 1989). The evidence for past discrimination against women as leaders is in the small number of female college presidents — fewer than 10 percent of the total in 1988 (Green, 1988a).

This discrimination itself leads to additional questions. Might the processes of presidential selection systematically exclude from consideration those thought to have a "feminine" orientation to leadership? Might professional socialization in a male-dominated profession require women to "think like men" if they are to be successful? Could ignoring the potential difference between men and women as leaders discriminate against those who do not conform to conventional wisdom, denying higher education a diversity of leadership approaches that might help to renew institutions?

Dangerous Myths, Helpful Mysteries

Five myths and three mysteries related to leadership in higher education were illuminated by ILP data. Myths are comforting. They provide a basis for action and belief when we otherwise do not know what to do. In a complicated world, myths are indispensable if we are to bring some semblance of order to our organizational life. But myths may also create significant problems for presidents by leading them to make poor judgments and reducing their effectiveness. Promulgating a presidential vision may inhibit the development of an authentic institutional voice. Trying to emulate the "best" style can lead presidents to try to be what they obviously are not, making them seem duplicitous and untrustworthy. Emphasizing distance may decrease presidential influence.

The most pernicious myths are those that call for charisma and transformation which, taken to extremes, may lead to the imperial presidency. They can cause presidents to see themselves as personally responsible for the college's survival and development, to insulate themselves from learning, and to initiate grand schemes that overpower the normal resilience of institutions and lead to damaging disruptions. Imperial presidents inflict leadership on their colleges.

Mysteries are helpful. They suggest that important matters should be treated as topics for discussion and inquiry, rather than accepted as dogma. They direct our attention to things that may be important but are usually overlooked. Examining the usefulness of teams may lead to reconsidering the college structures that affect the way we communicate and influence each other. Considering the effect of experience on leadership performance may change our views of who should be considered to fill the presidential role. And analyzing the relationship of gender to leadership from multiple perspectives may not only reveal new sources of presidential candidates who can capably fill demanding positions, but at the same time eliminate discriminatory practices that diminish rather than enhance the human spirit and subvert the essential and enduring functions of the academic enterprise.

CHAPTER 3

Recognizing
Effective Leadership

How can the effectiveness of leadership be depicted and evaluated, and what criteria should be used? These seemingly innocent questions turn out to be among the most vexing in leadership research.

Three Leadership Vignettes

It is difficult enough to assess the quality of leadership in most organizational settings, and it is particularly difficult in academic institutions. Brief descriptions of leadership scenarios, in three quite different organizations, will make clear why this is so.

The West Oshkosh Sturgeons

Frank Speaker has been the manager of the West Oshkosh Sturgeons Baseball Club for the past two seasons. Previously in the cellar, the Sturgeons finished sixth in the Winnebago League in Speaker's first season, and only three games out of the division championship in his second. Baseball is a game of statistics, and most indicators show that the Sturgeons have made remarkable progress. Because the team's record of wins and losses provides an objective benchmark and the rules of the game remain virtually unchanged, it might seem relatively easy to decide, based on that record, if Speaker is an effective leader. In fact, though, the situation is not clear cut, for as we look at it more closely, questions begin to multiply. Were the changes in the Sturgeons' performance due to Speaker's leadership, to changes of personnel through trades or injury, or to the players' maturation? Could the team's success be due to the weakening of its competition, not improvement by the Sturgeons? How much of a role has luck played? (They may have been in the cellar owing to some unlucky breaks, and of course, there is no place to go from the cellar but up.) Might Speaker's short-term decisions have strengthened the team this year, but at great cost for morale or effectiveness in the future? Clearly, many other factors may be at work, and it is difficult to know how much of the team's success is due to the manager. Nevertheless, most competent observers say with some confidence that Speaker is a good leader, and they have the team record to back up this judgment.

United Widget

Bea Strong is the CEO of United Widget, a private corporation manufacturing machine parts. Although there are some constraints on her corporate decisions, by and large she can decide whom to employ and what should be manufactured. Like Speaker, Strong has objective indicators of performance—in her case, they include her quarterly profit and loss statements. These indicators have remained essentially stable over the recent past. Some market analysts have suggested that the absence of improvement shows that Strong is not an effective leader. But unlike the relatively closed universe of Speaker, Strong's world is one of economic, political, and social changes which have major and unpredictable influences on the competitive position of her organization. The demand for widgets may be decreasing for reasons over which she has no control, and it may even be argued that, in United Widget's turbulent environment, maintaining quarterly profits at their current level is a worthy accomplishment. While some analysts believe Strong should boldly move the company away from a declining market in widgets to aggressively pursue state-of-the-art technology in doodads, others laud her for maintaining the widget-based institutional culture and having the company "stick to what it knows best." There is disagreement about whether Strong is a good leader, and the same data are used by both her admirers and her critics to support their positions.

Huxley College

Quincey Wagstaff is the president of Huxley College. When people look for objective evidence of the quality of his leadership, they have neither a win-lose record nor a balance sheet from which to make a judgment. To be sure, people can point to indicators such as changes in enrollment or funding levels, but then they quickly acknowledge that these do not measure the extent to which the college achieves its "real" goals, which are in large measure related to the personal and intellectual growth of students. However, people disagree about how progress toward these goals should be measured. Some think that scores of seniors on standardized examinations show the effectiveness of the college, but others believe that the outcomes of the Huxley experience become manifest only over the course of a lifetime and so cannot be assessed for at least a generation. In addition to the disagreement over how the college's goals are realized, Wagstaff faces several problems that are not confronted by the leaders in the other two setttings. Speaker and Strong decide who their employees shall be and, subject to labor and other contractual provisions, set their salaries. They decide what positions their employees should fill, and when their employees no longer perform adequately, they can trade or dismiss them. Wagstaff lacks these management options when dealing with most of his professional staff; indeed, *they* participated in *his* selection, and if they become dissatisfied with his leadership, they can influence his dismissal! Assessments of Wagstaff's leadership are likely to be related to whether or not he is seen as supporting the assessor's own particular interests. Because interests are diverse, outcomes are unclear, and Wagstaff's actions are sometimes equivocal, it is often possible to find some evidence to support every conceivable assessment of his leadership. As with Strong, there is disagreement as to whether Wagstaff is a good leader. Huxley College, however, is unlike United Widget in that there are few data that people agree are indicators of the "real purposes" of the organization.

The Problems of Leadership Assessment

These vignettes suggest the problems of assessing the effectiveness of leadership. For many organizations there is neither an agreed-upon definition of leadership nor a viable measure of it. Qualitative assessments depend on the values of the observer, the time period considered, and expectations based on institutional history. Using institutional performance as an index of leadership quality has always been problematic, and has become even more so today as environmental turbulence increases, organizational participants become more autonomous, and resource flexibility declines. Moreover, as Gardner (1990, p. 8) has pointed out, "leaders act in a stream of history. As they labor to bring about a result, multiple forces beyond their control, even beyond their knowledge, are moving to hasten or hinder the result. So there is rarely a demonstrable link between a leader's specific decisions and consequent events." Despite such difficulties, the relationship between leadership and institutional performance must still be examined. How can we judge a leader's success?

Studies of presidential leadership in higher education have come to grips with this question in a variety of useful ways. Three methods for identifying the quality of presidential leaders in higher education, used alone or in combination, appear with some frequency in the research to date. The first is based on the observations and judgments of experts who, in the absence of clear criteria for leadership, claim to "know it when they see it." The second depends upon nominations by peers based on reputation. The third relies on self-assessments by the leaders themselves.

Evaluations by Experts

To the extent that leadership is an art as much as a science, the evaluation of leaders by sophisticated and experienced experts has great merit. Experts can bring connoisseurship to their judgment and provide a holistic consideration which puts leaders in the context of an institution and its environment.

Assessments of this kind are often found in case studies of unusual institutions or programs when a researcher evaluates the part of a leader in creating or sustaining their distinctive features (see, for example, Keller, 1983; Gilley, Fulmer, and Reithlingshoefer, 1986; Green, Levine, and Associates, 1985; Perlman, Gueths, and Weber, 1988). Such studies are almost always historical. They usually examine institutions that have enjoyed unusual success or conspicuous failure, and attempt to relate unusual events or institutional changes to what are retrospectively taken to be the intended actions of presidents. But relating these changes to leadership is often problematic because it is difficult to differentiate what leaders have actually done from the myths and stories that have grown up around them. Moreover, case studies that examine successful or unsuccessful institutions and try to identify influential characteristics of their leaders pay no attention to instances in which leaders with similar characteristics faced different outcomes.

Judgments about the nature of good leadership may also be biased by the assessor's preconceptions and values. One expert may most readily see good leadership in a president who heals a wounded campus or renews an institution's culture, while another finds it more in a leader's potent strategy or ability to make tough and courageous decisions over strong opposition. Experts may be able to explain their judgments retrospectively, but they seldom specify in advance the criteria they use in sufficient detail to permit their assessments to be reproduced by others.

Evaluations by Peers

The assessment of leaders by peers has been the basis of several recent studies of leadership in higher education (see, for example, Vaughan, 1986; Roueche, Baker, and Rose, 1988). Presidents might appear to be well qualified to judge other presidents since they should presumably have special insight, based on their personal experience, into the complexities and demands of presidential life.

When presidents identify another president as an unusually effective leader, they are presumably responding to some visible aspect of the president's accomplishments. But much of what a president does takes place in the daily routines of institutional life, which are usually not visible from outside the campus. Few presidents can have more than a superficial sense of how another president functions in various institutional roles. In the absence of special personal knowledge, presidents may be prone to base their judgment of peers on symbolic factors not necessarily related to the effectiveness of the peers' leadership — for example, how well their colleagues speak at professional meetings, the size or reputation of their campuses, or whether they are personally well liked. It is probably no accident that lists of "best" presidents almost always include those who head the "best" colleges. This congruence is often taken as evidence that good leaders create good institutions, although it might just as plausibly reflect the reverse relationship — that good colleges create good presidents. And it should be no surprise that these lists frequently show that the "best" leaders work on larger campuses than the "average" leaders, with the exception of those at the elite liberal arts colleges. The finding that good presidents are likely to be located at the more prestigious and larger institutions suggests that presidential reputations may be based as much on visibility as on behaviors related to leadership.

Self-Evaluation

Self-evaluation asks leaders whom external observers or peers have identified as effective or ineffective, exemplary or average, to assess their own traits (see, for example, Fisher, Tack, and Wheeler, 1988). This approach is widely considered fraught with peril. Most people rate themselves more highly than others rate them. College presidents, for example, have been found on average (Birnbaum, 1986) to rate themselves as more effective than the average president and much more effective than their predecessors. They tend to see themselves as responsible for campus improvements and for campus events that have had positive effects, while denying their responsibility for campus events with negative consequences. Like most of us, they often ascribe their successes to their innate abilities and skills and their failures to the environment or bad luck.

Almost all presidents in the ILP, for example, considered themselves good leaders. In describing their "leadership style," they emphasized such terms as integrity, commitment, honesty, openness, fairness, concern for others, compassion, and vision. These self-assessments, all of them familiar ingredients of what is generally considered to be good leadership, appeared sincere and deeply felt. But the descriptions that others on their campuses gave of them were often less laudatory than, and sometimes diametrically opposed to, those that presidents gave of themselves. Discrepancies between what leaders say they do and what others see them as doing suggest that their self-assessments are biased by much the same cognitive processes that lead most of us to see ourselves more positively than others see us. In addition, it is not always clear whether self-reported data reflect leaders' perceptions of what they *actually* do, or what they think effective leaders *should* do. For example, when conventional wisdom says that good leaders have a vision, we should not be surprised to find that many leaders tell us — and believe firmly — that they have one.

Self-report data are rarely checked with a leader's constituents as they were in the ILP, so that it is usually impossible to know whether they reflect actual behavior or wishful thinking. And it should be added that even when studies based on self-evaluation present differences between "good" leaders and others that are "statistically significant," these differences are often so small as to be of no practical importance.

Leadership as Constituent Support

Because people differ in their view of what leadership is and what they expect leaders to do, there is not — nor is there likely ever to be — any single system for evaluating leadership that is universally accepted as valid and reliable. The best we can ask is that each study that examines leadership be explicit about its conceptual foundations; therefore, the remainder of this chapter is devoted to the concepts that shaped the ILP.

Some of the ideas on which the ILP was grounded have already been mentioned. The ILP considered leadership as a process of influencing perceptions of reality. Leadership influences people to focus their attention on specific stimuli and to interpret them in ways intended by the leader. Leadership is itself part of that interpreted reality and exists in the minds of its beholders (that is, its constituents). Good leadership is not defined by an ability to get subordinates to do something, but rather by a leader's effectiveness in making values and activities meaningful to others and developing a vocabulary to be used in communicating that meaning throughout the institution (Pondy, 1978). Good leadership is what its constituents believe it to be — and they don't always agree!

For any organization there are a large number of constituents or stakeholders (Mitroff, 1983) who are individuals and groups with some kind of relationship to the institution and who affect, and are affected by, its policies. Some institutional constituents in higher education are visible and known to everyone (for example, the faculty), while others may have only peripheral contact with the institution and remain largely unrecognized by most participants (for example, the suppliers of some goods and services). Some constituents (such as donors or legislatures) provide inputs into the institution, and some (such as employers of graduates or newspaper reporters) consume its outputs. Although all constituents, by definition, have the potential to affect the college, they differ in the frequency of their involvement and the importance of their influence. When a group has a major stake in the institution, it can be thought of as a strategic constituency.

One way of assessing the quality of presidential leadership is to determine whether the president enjoys the support of the institution's strategic constituencies. Constituency support can come about in a number of ways, and one group may support a president on grounds completely unrelated to — or even opposite to — those of another. Yukl (1981, p. 6) observes that "the selection of appropriate criteria of leader effectiveness depends on the objectives and values of the person making the evaluation. . . . When there are many alternative measures of effectiveness, it is usually an arbitrary decision as to which is the most relevant," and this is as true for colleges as for other organizations. How, then, can we select which criteria should be used?

The answer is not to distinguish criteria but simply to count constituencies. This assessment process takes a very complex question (What leadership behaviors lead to what outcomes desired by whom?) and substitutes in its place a relatively simple question (Does the president have the support of important constituencies?).

Defining leader effectiveness in terms of the extent to which strategic constituencies are satisfied is consistent with a cultural and interpretive view of organizations. In the absence of objective indicators, effectiveness, like leadership, is in the eyes of the beholder and depends on how well the organization is meeting whatever criteria each beholder has established (Pfeffer and Salancik, 1978). But while these particular assessments of effectiveness may be individual, they are not capricious; constituents must have reasons for maintaining their support. As Chaffee (1989b) has pointed out, constituent satisfaction is a particularly useful criterion of effectiveness because in some ways it incorporates both the goal and the resource models of effectiveness; constituents will be satisfied and continue their contributions to the organization if they see the organization pursuing the right goals and acquiring the resources it needs.

A leader who is able to command support of constituents, even when those constituents disagree on goals to be pursued or the resources necessary to achieve them, has met the needs of multiple and conflicting stakeholders and has a claim to be considered a good leader.

Leadership and Governance

Good leadership may depend on the support of constituents, but which ones? Although there are many strategic constituencies of a college — including students, alumni, legislators, suppliers, secondary schools, parents, employers, and community groups — probably most of us would agree that trustees, faculty, and administrative staff are the three most prominent. These groups are considered most frequently in both normative statements and research studies to be the major legitimate, continuing participants in institutional governance. They are the groups that presidents are presumed to lead. Many other groups, and students in particular, occasionally become involved in governance processes, but their participation is commonly more issue-specific and sporadic. They usually have little direct or continuous involvement with presidents and therefore less basis on which to make judgments of presidential performance. Presidents are frequently thought of as providing leadership to their boards, their faculties, and their administrations; they are seldom identified as leaders of their students.

From the perspective of governance, good leadership recognizes that college presidents must be simultaneously responsive to the three major constituencies. Even an ineffective president could enjoy the support of any one of these groups by making repeated concessions to it, and by slighting the interests of the other two. But a president who enjoys the support of all three has a claim to being a good leader. This claim is not based heavily on popularity (although popularity is not insignificant in the political environment of the academic campus), but more on the likelihood that these constituencies will have different interests and concerns. A good leader is one who has been able to balance these conflicting demands acceptably to these three critical constituencies, without merely currying favor or buying support. A brief look at each constituency will make clear why such a balance is sometimes difficult.

Trustee Support

The trustees represent the public. They are obligated to determine whether a president is responding effectively to community interests, using the institution's resources prudently and efficiently, representing the institution adequately to external groups, and implementing the board's policy directives accurately. Trustee support therefore represents the extent to which the president is seen as reflecting the will of the trustees and acting in a manner consistent with both the institution's and the public's interest. Trustees assess the president as the chief executive officer of the institution. When trustees support a president, they may say, as did one ILP trustee: "He is a good leader. He understands the principles of delegating. He is able to make decisions very easily. He does a good job in carrying these out. I call him a very brilliant guy. He seems to handle himself extremely well with other educational organizations. He seems to understand this educational business exceedingly well. He permits a freedom of action. He does not stifle the development of people or projects. He has done a good job."

Faculty Support

The faculty represent the institution's academic programs and its commitment to academic values. Faculty are obligated to judge whether the missions of the creation and dissemination of knowledge are being honored, whether a president is appropriately concerned with curriculum and student development, whether essential conditions for academic work are maintained, and whether the president operates in a manner consistent with a collegial community. Faculty support is based in part on their perception of the president's effectiveness as the institution's chief academic officer. A faculty member who supported an ILP president said: "One of her things is excellence in teaching and the extension of our services into the community at all levels. She is good at getting what we are doing out on the street. . . . Our working relationship is pretty open and constructive. I feel free to speak my mind to her. . . . She is an eloquent speaker, capable, well-informed. . . . She is well aware of much that is going on, . . . like the quality of education."

Administrative Support

The administration provides the structure and processes that support the institution's programs. Administrators know whether the president is a good manager who can make timely decisions, keep the college running smoothly, develop the potential of subordinates and engage them in institution building, and maintain a fair balance among the many conflicting interests of a complex bureaucracy. Administrative support indicates whether a president is a good chief operating officer. As one administrator who supported an ILP president put it: "He's tough and he has impact, but he's shrewd on the politics. He demonstrates openness, accessibility, rather than toughness. He's as good a CEO as I've ever seen. He has sheer intellect — he grasps things quickly, understands budgets and the financial side, has a unique sense and understanding of the academic content; he reads and holds seminars with senior people in areas he wants to understand."

The Three Strategic Constituencies

Although there may be considerable overlap in their views, each of the three strategic constituencies fills different roles, interacts with different aspects of the institution's environment, and therefore constructs different pictures of reality. The judgments of each constituent group about the president may be somewhat slanted because their perceptions are by necessity limited. But their synthesized views offer a comprehensive picture of a leader's ability to function effectively in the basic domains of institutional life. Presidents who satisfy one constituency are likely to find that it may consequently be more difficult to satisfy others (Pfeffer and Salancik, 1978). Therefore, a president who has the approval of trustees, faculty, and administrative colleagues has satisfied the basic interests of superiors (trustees) and subordinates (other administrators), as well as the interests of those who are engaged in the productive activity of the institution and who are in many ways outside its formal hierarchical structure (the faculty). Such a president can be said to be a good leader using the criterion of constituent support. The particular advantage of the strategic constituency model is that assessing good leadership does not require either determining the preferred goals of constituent groups or demonstrating agreement by these groups on the reasons for their support.

Determining Constituent Support

Fujita (1990) assessed the level of constituent support for ILP
presidents by analyzing the evaluative comments made in our
1986–87 interviews of trustees (usually the board chair and/or
one other trustee), faculty (usually the senate chair and either
the union president or one other faculty leader), and senior administrators (usually the academic and the administrative vice
presidents). All presidents were assessed by faculty and administrators. Trustee assessments were available for all but four presidents. Trustee support was assumed for presidents for whom
the information was unavailable. Of the thirty-two presidents,
sixteen were found to have support by all groups, and therefore could be considered good leaders using the criterion of constituent support. Ten were supported by two of the three groups,
and six were supported by only one or no group.

Fujita further found that both trustees and administrators commonly made positive assessments of their presidents and
that differences in constituent support were primarily due to
differing assessments by the faculty. Trustee assessments were
available for twenty-eight institutions, and all but two supported
the institutions' presidents. All but four of the thirty-two presidents were rated highly by their administrative colleagues. But
faculty ratings were quite different. Analysis of faculty support
(Birnbaum, 1992) found that, at the time of the first ILP visit,
sixteen of the thirty-two presidents were rated as good leaders
by the faculty. However, seven were given mixed ratings, and
nine were given low ratings.

In every ILP institution in which the president enjoyed
the support of the faculty, the president was also supported by
both trustees and administrators. If the ILP sample had been
larger, undoubtedly exceptions to this pattern would have been
found. For example, the recent history of higher education suggests that some presidents may gain short-term faculty support —
and often long-term martyrdom — by publicly challenging unpopular decisions of their trustees. Other presidents, on first entering office, may aggressively pursue restructuring programs
supported by faculty and trustees that lead to administrative dis-

affection. But for the ILP, faculty support was invariably accompanied by support of the other two groups.

Because of the high level of trustee and administrator ratings, the high correlation between faculty ratings and full constituency support, and the usefulness that faculty ratings proved to have in other parts of this study, this book will focus on faculty backing as the most significant measure of constituent support.

Characteristics Related to Leadership

The ILP collected three different categories of information to determine if they were related to the high, mixed, and low levels of presidential support in faculty assessments. The categories of institutional characteristics and personal characteristics are conventional and require only brief descriptions. The third category analyzed the ways the presidents thought, or their cognitive characteristics. These ideas about leaders' cognitive characteristics are not widely known, and they will be described in greater detail.

Institutional Characteristics

Since leadership occurs within a context, information was collected to describe a number of institutional characteristics that might have affected faculty perceptions of the president. The study design included eight institutions in each of four categories — universities, independent colleges, state colleges, and community colleges. The names and locations of these colleges are listed in Resource A. Other characteristics of institutions that were considered included governance auspices, size, wealth, the presence of faculty collective bargaining, and whether they were part of multicampus systems. In addition, during the initial visit to a campus the ILP researcher formed an impressionistic judgment as to whether the institution was "in crisis," a situation in which basic organizational functioning was threatened because of severe fiscal presssures, governance discontinuities, a jarring leadership succession, or external attacks on institutional quality or productivity. The distribution of colleges according to each of these factors is shown in Table 1, Resource C.

THE FAR SIDE   By GARY LARSON

"Well, we're lost. I knew from the start that it was just
plain idiotic to choose a leader based simply on the
size of his or her respective pith helmet.
Sorry, Cromwell."

Source: THE FAR SIDE © 1991 UNIVERSAL PRESS SYNDICATE.
Reprinted with permission. All rights reserved.

Personal Characteristics

The idea that leaders have certain characteristics or traits that
differentiate them from nonleaders is one of the oldest and most
thoroughly researched notions about leadership (Bensimon,
Neumann, and Birnbaum, 1989). In general, although some
traits and skills appear frequently to be characteristics of leaders

who are seen as effective, possession of such traits does not guarantee this effectiveness, nor does their absence proscribe it. This research tradition, doubtless because of its failure to discover dramatically meaningful patterns or relationships between traits and outcomes, is for all practical purposes no longer seriously pursued.

Nevertheless, the ILP chose to consider several personal characteristics either because they are commonly considered in research on leadership, or because they appeared to be specifically applicable to our focus on higher education. These characteristics included gender, length of tenure in office, whether the president had ever been a faculty member or an academic vice president, whether the president had previous presidential experience, and whether the president had been selected from inside or outside the institution. The distribution of ILP presidents on these factors is shown in Table 2, Resource C.

Cognitive Characteristics

This study, more than most examinations of academic leadership, put considerable emphasis on cognition—the ways leaders, and those influenced by leaders, think. Three concepts are of particular importance here—cognitive frames, strategy, and implicit leadership theories. The distribution of ILP presidents on these factors is described in Resource C.

Cognitive Frames. People use different lenses to observe and interpret, or "frame," their college world. These frames are conceptual maps for understanding an organization and interpreting the effectiveness of leaders' behavior. Frames focus the attention of individuals on one or another aspect of the organization and can also serve as cognitive blinders which leave what is "out of frame" unseen. Four such frames have been identified—bureaucratic, collegial, political, and symbolic (Bolman and Deal, 1984; Birnbaum, 1988a; Bensimon, 1989c; Bensimon, 1990b).

Leaders who see their role through a *bureaucratic* frame focus on an institution's structure and organization; a bureaucratic leadership frame emphasizes setting priorities, making orderly decisions, and communicating through established lines of authority. Leaders who employ a *collegial* frame focus on the achievement of goals through collective action; a collegial frame emphasizes building consensus, problem solving through a team approach, instilling loyalty and commitment to the institution, and leading by example. In using a *political* frame, leaders concentrate on monitoring internal and external environments and use influence to mobilize needed resources; a political frame emphasizes establishing relationships with important constituencies, developing coalitions of support, constructing compromises, and keeping lines of communication open. Leaders who view their functions through a *symbolic* frame give the institution meaning by interpreting its history, maintaining its culture, and reinforcing its values. Leaders emphasize a symbolic frame when they use language, myths, stories, and rituals to foster shared perceptions and beliefs.

Each of these frames gives leaders a distinctively different way of responding to organizational problems, and an examination of the way the frames function should provide insight into why leaders behave the way they do, and how they are seen by others.

Frames and Cognitive Complexity. Because each of the four frames focuses attention upon certain aspects of organizational life while slighting others, leaders who view their organizations through only one of the four are likely to have an unbalanced understanding of their institutions. When problems arise, a president who utilizes only a bureaucratic frame may immediately focus on a need for new rules. A dean who sees only through a collegial frame is likely to view problems — and solutions — in terms of group action and concern for people and to forgo, for example, an opportunity to reach others that would be clear to a leader using a symbolic frame. A senate chair who thinks that "it's all political" may be unable to see the serious structural issues that give rise to a specific institutional dilemma. Because people using single frames often have only single solutions for all situations, they may make numerous errors in judgment. In contrast, leaders who can call upon multiple frames have available to them alternative ways of considering problems and a repertoire of behaviors from which to choose. Leaders with multiframe perspectives can be thought of as "cognitively complex."

Strategy. Strategies influence the goals that organizational actors wish to achieve and the actions they believe will be most effective. Possessing strategic models, like using cognitive frames, makes it likely that individuals will see certain aspects of their environment as particularly important, and will be more likely to act in one way than another. Although strategy is usually described in terms of what people do, it is helpful for us to consider it here as a product of the way people think.

Chaffee (1985) identified three basic models of strategy: linear, adaptive, and interpretive. Linear strategists believe effective action results from rational decision making — gathering and analyzing data, formulating alternative actions, and projecting outcomes. They view goal accomplishment in a means-end fashion, focusing on internal factors and giving less attention to the environment than do other strategists. The linear strategist emphasizes improving efficiency.

Adaptive strategists believe in aligning their organizations with the environment, monitoring the environment for threats and opportunities, and changing the organization's programs to move into new environmental niches. The adaptive strategist emphasizes maintaining the flow of resources into the organization.

Interpretive strategists are concerned with how people see, understand, and feel about their organizations. They try to shape the values, symbols, and emotions influencing individual behaviors by explaining and clarifying organizational purpose. The interpretive strategist emphasizes changing perceptions so that others can find meaning in their organizational roles.

Implicit Leadership Theories. The concepts underlying presidents' views of leadership may affect their perceptions, behavior, and the way they define their role (Birnbaum, 1989a). Some presidents think of leadership as involving one-way communication through which they are expected to influence others, while other presidents see it as a two-way exchange, in which leaders and followers exert mutual influence. Presidents may define their role as determining goals and directing others toward achieving them or as helping others to establish their own goals and procedures. While some presidents may believe that it is best to evaluate their own achievements by assessing institutional performance, others say that they give primary attention to constituent reactions. Some presidents obtain information about their own performance passively through their participation in existing organizational communications networks, while others engage in active pursuit of information and reactions. And finally, some presidents indicate that they are able to use their intuition to understand how college events may be related to leader behavior.

Leadership and Institutional Change

Data about constituent support, institutional characteristics, and presidential characteristics and cognitive processes are based on materials collected during the initial visit to each of the thirty-two ILP campuses in 1986–87. Researchers returned to each institution in 1988–89, and through interviews, observations, and other data they collected, it was possible to assess how certain aspects of campus life had changed during the two-year period.

The presence of change is inevitable and unremarkable, and by itself says nothing about leadership. If change was random among the campuses, or if it appeared to be related to institutional characteristics that were beyond presidential control, it might make it more difficult to argue that, on average, presidents had some major effects on the fortunes of their institutions. Who the president was or what the president did might not have been very important.

But if changes were systematically related to constituent support, or to presidential or cognitive characteristics, it might indicate that presidents can make a difference, and suggest ways in which leaders could affect their institutions. The ILP studied five specific campus changes and conditions with which presidents could plausibly be associated. These included overall campus improvement as seen by the ILP researchers, changes in several critical areas of institutional functioning as seen by faculty, the degree to which presidents and faculties agreed on the extent of campus change, the level of campus stress, and changes in the level of resources available to the campus. These were selected because they were consistent with existing definitions of institutional effectiveness that focus on goal attainment, resource acquisition, and smooth internal functioning (Cameron, 1981), and because the data to determine them could be collected in the course of the research. Data describing levels of institutional change, and relating them to other presidential and institutional characteristics, are presented in Resource C.

Assessing Good Leadership

This chapter has developed a definition of good leadership in academic organizations based on constituent support. Constituent support is based on constituent perceptions and is therefore a criterion that is consistent with cultural and interpretive views of the meaning of leadership. Since the support of two strategic constituencies (trustees and senior administrators) was almost uniformly high, faculty ratings of their presidents were used as the indicator of constituent support. Only half of the presidents enjoyed high faculty support, and several institutional, personal, and cognitive characteristics appeared related to their support level. These relationships are described in greater detail in Resource C. Following is a summary of some of the more interesting findings.

Faculty support of a president was generally unrelated to institutional factors, although there was a modest and negative association with unionization and with system membership. This suggests that some structural elements may make leadership more difficult, albeit not impossible. There was also a tendency for faculty to give less support to their presidents when their colleges were neither rich nor poor. It may be that faculty in relatively rich institutions had the resources they needed, and faculty in relatively poor institutions had learned how to live with less. In either case, the president may have been seen as having relatively little influence over resource allocation. Perhaps it is when institutions are neither rich nor poor that resources become an object of contention, presidential decisions cannot please everyone, and institutional success at resource acquisition becomes a proxy for the quality of leadership.

Most personal characteristics of presidents were unrelated to the level of faculty support they enjoyed, but one factor was of great importance. New presidents had a much higher level of support than did old presidents. Although it might have been predicted that presidents would get better with experience, and therefore increase their faculty support, exactly the opposite appeared to occur. Later chapters will explore this phenomenon in some depth.

The ways in which presidents talked about leadership, communication, or assessing outcomes seemed unimportant. But the strategies they followed, and the cognitive models they were seen by others as employing, did make a difference. Presidents using only interpretive strategy were highly supported, while those using either linear or adaptive strategy were not. Presidents seen by others as cognitively complex and using multiple models to understand problems were more highly supported than those who were not perceived as cognitively complex.

Institutional changes over two years were for the most part only modestly related to institutional or presidential characteristics. The factors that seemed most related to change were the same factors that were most closely associated with faculty support. Positive changes were most evident when presidents were new to their office, were cognitively complex, and used interpretive strategy. Presidents had the most negative impact on changes when they used linear strategy.

In a world in which social reality is interpreted and constructed, it is possible to create a plausible schema of relationships — indeed, to construct many alternative schemas — from almost any data set. Most readers who browse through the data in Resource C will be able to develop many interesting ideas about college leadership. But being able to identify some potentially interesting factors related to presidents and their institutions does not necessarily make it possible to generalize about leadership with any certainty, or to propose cause and effect relationships with any confidence.

A major part of this analytic problem may be that quantifying and summarizing certain elements of colleges and of leadership has ignored a central proposition — that leadership is dependent on context. Although there may have been few changes on average at the ILP institutions that could be associated with leadership, there may have been significant changes in specific cases. Perhaps leadership *does* have generalizable qualities, but these properties are not discoverable through analyses that use abstractions to look at institutions collectively. They must instead be gleaned through concrete examples that examine individual institutions holistically.

The data discussed in this chapter have provided some enticing clues about what to look for. Presidential term, cognitive complexity, and interpretive strategies, for example, may prove to be useful ideas that can help provide a better understanding of leadership, constituent support, and campus change in specific institutions. These possibilities are explored in Part Two.

PART TWO

Sources of
Effective Leadership

CHAPTER 4

Presidents and Faculty Support

The previous chapter presented several presidential characteristics that appeared to be associated with both faculty support and campus change. However, it was not clear how these characteristics could be put together into sensible and coherent patterns. The single most important presidential characteristic was whether a president was new (had been in office for less than three years at the time of the first campus visit, with an average tenure of 1.7 years) or old (had been in office for five or more years, with an average tenure of 12.7 years). Seventy-five percent of new presidents, but only 25 percent of old presidents, enjoyed high faculty support, and the colleges of new presidents were much more likely than those of old presidents to be judged by ILP researchers, as well by faculty, to have improved.

The presidency is a complex leadership role, and it might be reasonable to expect that presidents would become more proficient as they gained experience in office. Blau (1973) has endorsed this proposal, suggesting that presidents who remain in office for many years probably do so because their leadership has been successful. But the relationships described in Chapter Three suggest just the opposite; to the extent that faculty support is a measure of effective leadership, new presidents enjoy more support than old presidents. Why did faculty rate new presidents so positively and old presidents so negatively?

Some answers to this question were developed through a case-by-case study of the relationships between faculty and the thirty-two ILP presidents who were in office during the initial campus visit in 1986–87 (Birnbaum, 1992). For each campus, a case report was compiled from the materials collected during the two campus visits. Typically, each case report was based on interviews with approximately twelve trustees, administrators, and faculty in formal leadership positions during the first campus visit, and another twelve in the second. Institutions were examined for patterns of similarities and differences that could throw light on the differing levels of faculty support for old and new presidents.

Faculty Support for New Presidents

Of the sixteen new presidents, twelve had high faculty support, two had mixed support, and two had low support.

High Faculty Support

The twelve new presidents with high faculty support led institutions of different types, faced different problems, and took different actions. But despite this, they proved to have a number of characteristics in common.

In a variety of ways the faculties of these colleges held clearly negative views of the new president's predecessor. Of the eleven predecessors for whom data were available, three were reported as having been fired by their boards and were depicted as autocratic, isolated from or belittling of the faculty, or administratively incompetent. Five others had poor faculty relationships ranging from contention to open warfare. The faculty described them in pungent terms: one was "a model of what a president ought not to be — old, staid, had no contact with the faculty, didn't want to make changes"; another, "double-dealing and dishonest, more appropriate to a corporate board room"; a third, "a crook with the morals of a street criminal, [who had] an active network of spies and brought out the very worst in academic conduct." Three other predecessor presidents had apparently been well thought of earlier in their careers, but when they left office were seen as burned out, faced with problems they could not handle (for example, a president who was socially adept but could not deal with emerging financial crises), or locally "bogged down" and obviously job-hunting. As a consequence, faculty morale had been low under these predecessors, and without exception, the succession process had led to faculty perceptions of increased campus well-being and a more favorable faculty view of the new presidents. As one faculty leader put it, after the new president was appointed, "faculty morale went up because the former president was considered weak. There was no agony when the previous president left."

Faculty at these institutions felt that progress had stalled under the previous president. They had high expectations about what the new president would be able to do, expressed a hope for strong leadership, and deferred criticism during the early part of the new president's term. New presidents could sense this anticipation. One said, "There was a lot of expectation in the college that we needed to move forward, and this was not happening under my predecessor. People were poised to go to work, almost saying, 'Tell me what to do to move the college forward.'" Even where the president took dramatic action, the faculty withheld criticism. As one new president explained, "Everyone there had a sense that something needed to be done differently, so I was given the opportunity to show I was doing the right things before being judged."

Most of these new presidents were selected through procedures involving search committees, which generally included faculty. To some extent, therefore, these presidents were seen as having been chosen by the faculty. Furthermore, in faculty eyes, faculty participation had continued once the new president's term had started. Although the approaches of these new presidents varied from highly consultative to rather directive, all the presidents were seen as seeking real input from the faculty and supporting faculty participation in governance. A faculty leader on a campus with a new president considered good about consultation said, "Our president is open and seeks input from the faculty and staff, and she actually does something with the input she gets. Not like the previous president who asked for recommendations but did not use them." A faculty member with a more directive new president commented that while the previous administration had belittled the faculty, the new administration "listens to the faculty; they don't always agree, but you're listened to and respected."

The new presidents were faculty oriented in another way as well. Most of them spent a great deal of time and energy learning about their new institutions and, in particular, what the faculty expected of them. This sometimes took the form of campus visits after their selection but prior to their formal appointment, meeting with every faculty department, identifying the faculty leadership and consulting with them, or on smaller campuses, meeting individually with every member of the faculty. As a consequence, as one faculty member expressed it, "I was impressed with [the new president's] desire to identify with the faculty leadership. He was clearly interested in finding out what the faculty thought."

These presidents were all putting time and energy into useful activities, and all were seen as action oriented although their actions differed. In some cases, they had taken dramatic steps to restructure the institution, to change senior administrators, to develop strategic plans, or to take charge of marketing and community relations activities. In others, they were devoting extraordinary time and energy to specific problems seen by the faculty as important, such as fund-raising or recruitment. These moves were accepted as a welcome departure from an unresponsive predecessor. Quick action was interpreted as vigorous and decisive leadership. If a president chose instead to defer immediate decisions while seeking further consultation, this, too, was praised as reflecting thoughtful consideration and an understanding of institutional culture.

Completing the favorable picture, these new presidents were seen as supporting and having confidence in their faculties. In return, faculty usually saw the president as committed to the institution and to faculty well-being. As a consequence, said a faculty leader, the selection of the new president gave us "a new direction, a new sense that we are working together. She has done a lot to get rid of apathy."

Mixed or Low Faculty Support

Because there were only four new presidents who received mixed or low faculty support, generalizations are difficult. All had predecessors who did not enjoy the support of the faculty, and two had been fired. Only one new president had been selected through an open search.

Our informants considered all four campuses to be facing financial or political crises, although their financial situations were not necessarily any more desperate objectively than those at other institutions where presidents enjoyed high support. At each of the four colleges, the new presidents took a specific action, with little or no faculty consultation, that aroused strong faculty disapproval. Their actions were primarily rational responses to specific organizational dilemmas — that is, consistent with the bureaucratic frame (for example, changing faculty personnel policies to accommodate a budget deficit); but in faculty eyes, the responses gave little or no consideration to the collegial or cultural campus patterns.

In the two cases of mixed support, faculty perceptions of the new president were split. At one institution, the new president had taken drastic steps to balance the budget, including layoffs, restructuring, and new programs. Faculty leaders disagreed on whether the changes were good or bad. At the other, a new president had quickly developed a reorganization plan and removed individuals judged unqualified. The faculty supported the substance of the plan but were concerned about the process that was followed. As one faculty leader said, "It created much concern about how it was done. . . . It caused quite an uproar. Some felt not enough faculty and student input had been sought."

Both instances of low faculty support involved the promotion of long-time administrators whose assumption of the presidency had not resulted from an open search with faculty participation and was therefore seen as lacking legitimacy from its inception. Neither president was viewed by faculty as taking any focused actions upon assuming office or having any particular programmatic interests. One president was seen as autocratic, relying too much on charisma and failing to consult.

A faculty leader called the other "a pragmatist without an agenda. Right now, the president has no credibility — is there but is not doing anything except what is absolutely necessary."

Faculty Support for Old Presidents

Of the sixteen old presidents, four had high faculty support, five had mixed faculty support, and seven had low faculty support. As was true with new presidents, old presidents were also likely to have been selected by committees with faculty representation and to have succeeded predecessors who did not enjoy faculty support, although data on both points were more difficult to obtain and interpret because so many years had elapsed.

High Faculty Support

Four old presidents enjoyed the support of their boards, administrative colleagues, and faculty. Their institutions differed considerably in size, program, and control, but there were certain elements that uniformly described them. Although one or more of these elements were also seen among presidents without high faculty support, only presidents with high support had them all.

Old presidents with high support were judged by their faculty leaders as being both technically competent and concerned with people as well as organizational tasks. Comments such as "he's an excellent manager of the budget" were coupled with "he has, from the day he became president, articulated that the most important thing is people." This concern for people could be accompanied by personal warmth, but did not have to be. Even presidents with high support who were also seen as somewhat aloof were identified as sensitive to the human dimensions of college life.

The presidents were seen as honoring and working within established governance structures, accepting faculty participation in decision making, and being concerned with process. Whether dealing with senates or unions, their willingness to support and work within the existing system was unquestioned by the faculty. A typical faculty comment was, "The president is

committed to collegiality and shared governance. The faculty
here have a major role in decision making. . . . The president
doesn't go around faculty leadership."

Old presidents with high faculty support were described
as having a strong sense of values that was consistent with the
purposes and missions of the institution but at the same time
transcended them. Each was an ardent advocate of the institution but saw the college mission not as a managerial goal but
as a means to achieve some larger purpose such as the advance-
ment of knowledge, the provision of educational opportunity,
community service, or the inculcation of ethical values.

They were totally involved with their campuses but did
not attempt to micromanage them. As one faculty member said,
"He does not get lost in the minutiae, yet he is interested in the
nooks and crannies of the institution." Presidential involvement
was seen by the faculty as a symbol of expertise, dedication,
and a commitment to give precedence to institutional over personal well-being. Such a president "takes a proprietary interest
in this college, he keeps abreast of everything. The college is
his life. There is very little self-interest in him. He is not looking to make a name for himself outside this institution."

These presidents were seen as people who were "very fair
and ethical," as having "high integrity and competence, not dictatorial or heavy handed." They kept promises once made, were
not afraid to tackle controversial problems, stated their positions, and were not seen as having hidden agendas. As a consequence, they were described as principled, decent, honest, and
trustworthy; and faculty reported that "there is little distrust that
the administration is cooking up something."

While these presidents were seen as respecting the faculty,
listening to them, and being responsive to their concerns, they
were also willing to make difficult and controversial decisions,
and occasionally to take actions contrary to the expressed will
of the faculty. These presidents actively sought information and
initiated communication. Faculty would say, for example, "She
is willing to listen. She goes out of her way to seek information
and alternatives and to listen to more than one source before
reaching a conclusion." At the same time, these presidents main-

tained the prerogative to act contrary to expressed faculty views, and each had done so on important matters. As one faculty leader said, "We have an accommodative relationship, but he never gives up the store; that is, he never gives up the management prerogative." When these presidents acted contrary to the faculty will, they did so in a manner that reflected their respect for the faculty and for the process. One faculty leader, for example, said that the president rarely vetoes faculty actions, but "if he does, he first comes back and tells us why and opens the door for further discussion." These presidents were able to act contrary to faculty views without resentment because "this does not happen often. He has such a legacy of good will, people are able to accept it."

The presidents were seen as emphasizing the positive rather than the negative aspects of the campus, and building on strengths rather than emphasizing weakness. Faculty comments that "he has a positive notion of what it means to be a leader, not a negative notion" referred to the way such a president "engenders and reinforces commitment from the people here," influencing them through persuasion and not through rules or coercion. Finally, these presidents were personally liked and admired and were seen as neither overbearing nor officious.

Mixed or Low Faculty Support

The characteristics of old presidents with mixed support were similar in many ways to those with low support, and the line between them was often difficult to draw. These twelve presidents could be placed on a continuum where the extremes were clear, but where the differentiation in the middle ranges was less so. On the five campuses with mixed support, faculty either were split in their assessment of the president or described a love-hate relationship in which they acknowledged that the president, although flawed as a leader, had made significant contributions to the college. Although criticisms were many, faculty reaction to the president was more likely to be indifference or resigned acceptance than animosity. The dominant faculty hope was not that the president would leave, but that the president would improve. For example, a faculty leader on one campus described his president as "not much loved, but he is respected because of [his] narrowly defined objectives rather than vision. Whatever faculty grousing occurs about the lack of faculty participation, they agree the administration has done a good job." On another campus, a faculty leader described the president as "authoritarian and autocratic, but he has been quite effective. The college is better off now than it would have been under the leadership of another president."

On the seven campuses with low faculty support, perceptions of presidential weaknesses were not offset by a belief that the presidents had improved their campuses. Instead, it was frequently stated that the president had inhibited institutional development. Faculty-president relationships were contentious, and the dominant faculty desire was not that the president would improve, but that the president would leave. At four of these campuses, presidents who had lost faculty support still maintained the support of their boards and administrative colleagues. But at three others, the president had lost the support of one of these groups as well. At one such campus, a faculty leader said, "There has been a leadership problem here for years. The president is in over his head. He has been a complete failure. There are few faculty here who have confidence in the president's ability to do his job."

Nine of the twelve presidents with mixed or low faculty support were criticized as being authoritarian. Although the particular mix of characteristics differed from campus to campus, a composite picture was that of presidents whose emphasis was on achieving tasks, with little or no concern for people. These presidents were variously criticized as being impatient with process, being indifferent to faculty participation in governance, micromanaging specific institutional processes or programs, acting too quickly with little or no faculty consultation, being aloof or cold, failing to communicate adequately, being difficult to deal with, not suffering fools gladly, or being unpredictable. Some were criticized for emphasizing management systems and failing to take account of the human side of the organization, while others were criticized for avoiding management systems so they could insert themselves into any decision they wished and act with no limitations on their discretion. In either case, they were seen as directive and controlling, and faculty were described as fearful or withdrawn as a consequence. One typical view was that "the faculty are dissatisfied. It's a very intimidated faculty. There is a lot of secrecy here. The president is not in close contact. He is highly controlling of communication channels. He is unnecessarily unwilling to let others participate in decision making. Some people saw goals coming down by fiat versus having the faculty help formulate them."

The three presidents not seen as authoritarian were criticized for being passive. Although they entered their institutions with high faculty expectations, they were no longer seen as major players on campus. One such president was described as "slow in considering ideas. I think he is weak as a leader. I don't see him as setting the institution in a certain direction." Of another it was said, "He does not present many initiatives. He is not much of a leader; he does not get involved, and when he does, it is in flashes — and those don't come often. He doesn't show people that he cares about what they are doing." These passive presidents shared certain characteristics with authoritarian presidents; they were seen as insensitive to faculty criticism, defensive, and unwilling to consult widely. However, while authoritarian presidents emphasized task and ignored relationships, passive presidents seemed concerned with neither.

How President-Faculty Relationships Develop

Among the thirty-two ILP institutions, three-quarters of all new presidents, but only one-quarter of all old presidents, enjoyed high faculty support. Old and new presidents may look quite different, but in fact they may be simply displaying two different stages in a presidential career. Data drawn from both groups should illuminate patterns that describe the development of president-faculty relationships over time. The five circumstances presented below describe what new presidents generally face when they first arrive on campus. They include faculty dissatisfaction with the former president, initial faculty support for the newcomer, pressure to take action, an atmosphere conducive to increasing communication, and an expectation of good leadership. Chapter Five will propose a coherent and plausible explanation of how and why, after this common beginning, presidential tenures move in different directions that have major consequences for the presidents' ability to provide leadership.

Faculty Dissatisfaction with the Former President

The ILP data indicate that at the time a presidential vacancy occurs, faculty leaders are typically dissatisfied with their parting president. All presidencies begin with a vacancy created by the leave-taking of a predecessor, and it is likely that the predecessor did not have the confidence of the faculty. The case reports of nineteen campuses included comments on the quality of the predecessor. Of these, comments about sixteen reflected a poor rating, and on just three, a good rating. Comments about predecessors on the other thirteen campuses were unclear or missing. Poor ratings were given to predecessors who were described with words such as autocratic, widely disliked, not respected, arbitrary, an absolute and utter disaster, ineffective, dictatorial, or the like. Predecessors were disparaged for being the cause of poor morale, being unable to balance a budget, causing a rupture of college-community relations, or drawing rigid lines between faculty and administration. At best, they were seen as leaving their institutions drifting; at worst, their campuses were described as battlefields. Several were identified as having been fired. A faculty leader said of one, "He was as qualified to run an institution of higher education as an earthworm. For most of his term here there was misdirection and chaos. The faculty was oppressed. He governed by fiat."

The ratings of predecessor presidents provide support for the belief that most presidents are not well regarded by their faculties at the time they leave office. Faculty pleasure with the predecessor's leaving may range from quiet satisfaction to elation, as on the ILP campus where a faculty leader said, "We felt like 'ding dong, the wicked witch is dead' when he left."

Initial Faculty Support for the New President

Initial faculty support for an incoming president is high for several reasons; the faculty constituency has participated in the selection process, dissatisfaction with the previous president makes any change seem desirable, and the new president is seen as possessing attributes that will act as a corrective for the perceived weaknesses of the previous president.

The arrival of a president on a campus is an event with major significance both for the institution and the individual. For the institution, it is the culmination of a lengthy process that has functioned to meet a number of organizational needs (Birnbaum, 1988b). Although the ILP did not check on the matter systematically, it appears that search committees with faculty representation participated in most selection processes. The elaborate processes of these committees are designed, in part, to certify the high quality of the candidate eventually selected, and participation in the selection of a leader is apt to increase the initial support of that leader (Hollander, 1987).

Just as faculty tend to blame the previous president for many of the current problems of the campus, so they see the arrival of a new president as a solution to those problems. The case reports suggest that committees actively search for — or retrospectively report that a part of the appeal of the replacement president is — perceived strengths in areas in which the previous president was conspicuously weak, a finding consistent with the conclusions of other scholars (Walker, 1977; Kauffman, 1980). It may also be that over time the faculty come to believe that different presidential abilities are now called for. After an aggressive entrepreneur, there may be a desire for someone who is conservative and cautious. A tough manager can create a desire for a strong academician; an externally oriented president, for one who will focus on the campus. The new appointee is welcomed by the campus community and particularly by the faculty who were dissatisfied with the previous president. The campus mood at the time a new president is named typically ranges from enthusiasm to euphoria.

The succession process also has consequences for the new appointee. While almost all new presidents have held significant administrative positions in higher education, few (six of thirty-two in the ILP) had prior presidential experience. The elation of the campus is often matched by the excitement of the new president, who has finally achieved a position that marks the apex of an administrative career. If newly appointed presidents had harbored lingering doubts about their competence, achievements, or judgment, these are now dissipated in the flush of succession. Their appointment offers objective confirmation of their accomplishment. College presidencies are positions of great status in our society. There are no more than 3,200 of them at one time. The new president can take justifiable pride in joining America's elite.

New Presidents Take Action

New presidents arrive on campuses facing difficult problems for which their successors were unable to provide suitable answers, and are under pressure to move quickly and take actions that symbolize a change in leadership. For the campus, the new president is a fresh start — a symbol that "there is a new direction, a new sense that we are working together, . . . a new sense that we are moving." An administrator commented, "Having a new president is like opening a window. It raises hopes — all those feeling oppressed view a new president as another chance. Expectations rise, and there are subsequent expectations for visible outcomes."

Faculty and other campus constituencies expect that the new president will make decisions and take actions that confirm their judgment in supporting the appointment. Presidents, in turn, realize that their first acts may have a profound effect on their terms of office and strive to develop an image of skill and decisiveness. One said, "The most crucial part of the presidency is the first few months; the first statements you make will set the overall pace and tone." During this time, presidents are likely to articulate statements about institutional missions, begin administrative restructuring, initiate strategic planning activities, or engage in similar dramatic acts that symbolize the fact that they have "taken charge" (Bensimon, 1987). Presidents who do not take such actions may initially be viewed with concern by the faculty who may ask themselves, "Is she capable? In charge? I questioned whether she was strong enough, if she was ricocheting from one crisis to another. When she first came here there was a feeling of relief. But then there were concerns about her leadership. She didn't make decisions, get things into shape." Such concerns can be allayed by firm actions taken later that permit faculty to retrospectively interpret the delay as a thoughtful approach to problem solving.

New Presidents Increase Communication

New presidents try to make sense of a new environment by initiating and responding to communications with various segments of the campus community. This involvement leads new presidents to be seen as responsive to the interests of others.

Presidents are very visible during their first months on the job as they spend time touring the campus, receiving delegations, consulting with campus participants, asking questions, and seeing and being seen. This heightened activity level symbolizes the arrival of new leadership and helps the president understand institutional patterns and make sense of a strange and unfamiliar environment (Bensimon, 1987). Some presidents may engage in these activities primarily as a tactic to increase their own influence; others may consider it part of a strategy to increase their own understanding. Regardless of their motives, their initial activities significantly increase the level of campus communications. One faculty leader commented, "Lots of memos go back and forth. This new administration is much more open than the old one." Another said, "People feel free to make suggestions. That is the big difference between the new president and her predecessor. Things are much more open. There is a flow of communication, both up and down." Presidents are likely during this early part of their term to publicly profess a consultative style, and to formally communicate to the campus their desire to receive input and their openness to both criticism and support. Their efforts at communication are rewarded by initial faculty perceptions of presidential openness, skill, and commitment.

New Presidents Receive Praise

During the early phases of their terms, presidents are likely to hear more praise than criticism of their actions as they reorganize structures and initiate new programs. Potential criticism of a new president is muted because the expectation of good leadership overwhelms any evidence to the contrary (the so-called honeymoon period). Faculty have a vested interest in believing that the new president is successful because it justifies their previous opposition to the predecessor and confirms the importance of their participation in the selection process. Support may be based on substance, but it often depends as much on the expectations and hopes of others and their willingness to suspend critical judgment. One president, describing his first actions, commented, "I had a window of opportunity to take actions. This was because people here were feeling that the college had been in times of difficulty. There was a feeling that decisions should be made no matter what they might be — that there should not be the need to put everything through a microscope."

In addition, as new presidents go from forum to forum, and problem to problem, their responses are initially seen as individual events, and faculty do not yet know enough to put them into a context or interpret them. The meanings of the president's actions are unclear while the actions are being observed serially, and it takes time for enough information to be collected so that they can be understood retrospectively. Campus coalitions that might have formed under normal circumstances to criticize presidential initiatives are temporarily silenced because of the organizational disruption caused by the succession process. Until the president has done enough to clarify the course of the administration, it is difficult for others to construct a coherent and meaningful interpretation of the president's actions that will enable them to know where their potential allies are.

Initial Stages of Presidential Terms

These five general propositions indicate that most ILP presidents followed predecessors with low faculty support, began their own terms of office with high support, increased communications, received praise, and were expected by the campus to act in ways that confirmed their new roles — all factors that should have helped to promote a successful presidential term. But common beginnings did not necessarily lead to common outcomes. In Chapter Five, we will consider how and why some presidents continued to enjoy high faculty support as they matured in office, while others did not.

CHAPTER 5

Why Presidents Succeed or Fail

We have seen that while presidents appear to begin their terms in similar ways, they end them with varying degrees of faculty and constituent support. A study of the thirty-two ILP institutions suggests that presidents follow one of three different paths, which may be called the modal presidency, the failed presidency, and the exemplary presidency. This chapter will describe these different paths and consider why presidents succeed or fail as college leaders.

The Path of the Modal Presidency

The modal presidency is just that: the typical or average presidency which begins with high support from all constituencies and ends with support by trustees and administrators, but not faculty. Why do these presidents lose faculty support?

Chapter Four showed that new presidents typically take aggressive actions early in their terms which symbolize the arrival of new leadership, and during this honeymoon period, faculty are likely to accept — or at least not to overtly criticize — the president's actions. Presidents in general are likely to believe that they are superior to their predecessors and that they are the instruments of positive campus change (Birnbaum, 1986), and at least during the early days of their terms, they are likely to receive explicit messages from others that reinforce this predilection. Ironically, it is these initial successes that sow the seeds of diminishing faculty support.

The Consequences of Success and Certainty

Initial successes and the withholding of criticism lead modal presidents to become more certain of themselves, to overestimate their effectiveness, to become less sensitive to complaints, and to diminish two-way communications. During the honeymoon period, presidents can do little wrong; constituents who support a president's actions are quick to say so, and any who are troubled are apt to watch and wait rather than speak up. But all too soon, new presidents are no longer "new." Constituents become less likely to give the president the benefit of the doubt, or to excuse presidential judgments with which they disagree on the grounds that the president is not yet familiar with the campus. The press of routine obligations, as well as the need to attend to the sporadic crises of institutional life, make it difficult for presidents to continue to engage in the processes of interaction and discussion that marked the first phases of their terms. As one administrative leader said, "You can't keep up the pace; the honeymoon ends; people's oxen get gored." Unrealistic expectations go unfulfilled, and faculty say, "When the new president came in we were euphoric, hoping for real change. I'm dissatisfied, even though compared to the previous president, it's much better."

Presidents who initially communicated with faculty in order to make sense of institutional life now feel less need to do so. They are more willing to develop, and have more confidence in, their own interpretations based on their increasing experience. As faculty criticism develops, it may be discounted by modal presidents as coming from unrepresentative cabals or stoically accepted as reflecting an unfortunate but inescapable consequence of firm leadership. The modal presidential view is that friends come and go, but enemies accumulate. As one president said, "The longer you stay, the more mistakes you make; you make enemies, and you take more risks that scare people. The president's principal responsibility is to make decisions."

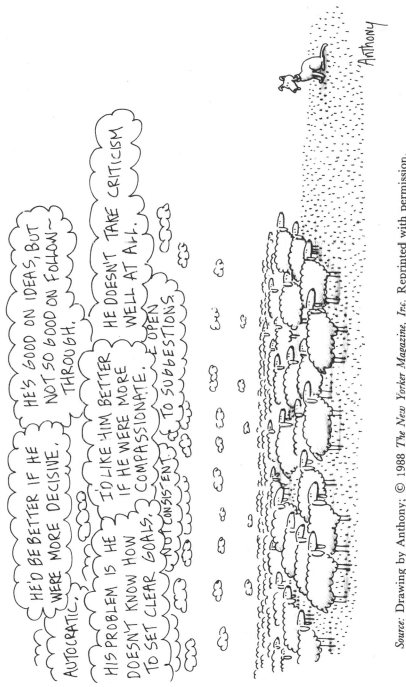

Source: Drawing by Anthony; © 1988 *The New Yorker Magazine, Inc.* Reprinted with permission.

This withdrawal from soliciting and responding to faculty influence is often so gradual that it may go unnoticed by the president and even be denied when pointed out because it is inconsistent with presidential self-perceptions. Presidents will publicly reaffirm their commitment to listen to others even as their faculties complain that they do not do so. Sometimes modal presidents act in ways that discourage faculty communication. They may be seen as remote: "The president is difficult to approach; he does not seem to have a comprehension of some of the concerns or problems of the lower echelon." Or they may be beyond influence: "He is directive. He has definite ideas on whatever his goals are at the moment, and if you don't agree he can be vindictive. If you are opposed to his ideas, a couple of years later when you want something you won't get it because he will be mad at you." As a result, faculty unhappiness goes underground, and presidents may be misled by the appearance of smooth operations and lack of conflict into believing that they enjoy faculty support.

As communication diminishes, the modal president comes to be viewed by faculty leaders as indifferent to faculty interests. Faculty may increasingly believe that the modal president does not seek advice, ignores advice that is inconsistent with the president's own predilections, fails to attend to faculty concerns, or in other ways indicates a lack of respect for faculty. As one faculty leader described it, "The upper administration is pretty remote. There is no opportunity for give and take. It is difficult to have access to the president. They are thin-skinned about criticism. People lower their voices when they criticize the administration. The administration would be surprised to know this; they would be hurt and then angry. Many people have retreated into their own bailiwicks."

When criticisms like this are brought to their attention, modal presidents may come to believe that faculty are being irresponsible, that faculty leaders are not truly representative, and that as presidents they must ignore petty carping and become even more assertive if the institution is to make progress. They may begin to stress some of the characteristics that our culture commonly associates with good leadership, such as certainty, courage, distance, and willingness to decide, making it even more difficult for them to appreciate alternate views or to change.

Changing Patterns of Communication

As modal presidents gain experience, they communicate and respond more to trustees and other administrators than to faculty. College problems are often created by changes in the external environment related to matters such as resource acquisition or political support. Both the nature of the problems and the planning of solutions are likely to be proposed or defined by trustees or other senior administrators, and presidents find themselves spending more time responding to their trustees, coordinating boards, and administrative colleagues and less time with the faculty. Faculty leaders see this happening and conclude that even when faculty are consulted it is usually a *pro forma* exercise to provide a patina of legitimacy. On one campus, a faculty leader said, "The administration often seems reticent to discuss things before making a decision. Lots of times when the president and vice president are considering decisions, they involve the faculty after the fact, when the faculty could have had input from the beginning. The faculty feels it's a waste of time, and the college is deprived of important information."

When more pointed communication with faculty takes place, it is often in response to difficulties initiated by faculty who are disgruntled; faculty who are content are less likely to seek the president's attention or publicly proclaim their satisfaction with presidential performance. The president is thus likely to interact disproportionately with activists and dissidents. Presidential enthusiasm and energy can be quickly eroded by the constant press of college life and by the belief that one's efforts may not be truly appreciated by the faculty.

As modal presidents find less fulfillment in their relationships with faculty, they take increasing comfort in their administrative colleagues. One of the first acts of most new presidents is to restructure the college's administration, in order to create reporting lines and structures familiar to them and develop their own teams. The new senior administrators, who owe their positions to the president and who actively participate in developing the policies to which the faculty now object, bolster the president's sense of competence even as faculty backing diminishes. This tendency for leaders and their teams to reinforce each other's views, isolate themselves from disconfirming evidence, and become increasingly rigid and resistant to change is not unique to colleges and has been noted in other organizational settings (Katz, 1982; Pfeffer, 1983; Finkelstein and Hambrick, 1990).

Furthermore, modal presidents may retain the support of their boards and colleagues even as they lose the support of the faculty, because the three groups employ different criteria to assess presidential effectiveness. While ILP trustees were most likely to assess presidents on the basis of their perceived competence and commitment and administrators based judgments on competence and involvement, the faculty looked to the president's willingness to be influenced and respect for the institution's culture (Fujita, 1990). Thus, it may be the same administrative acts that lead trustees and administrators to see the modal president as competent that prove to the faculty that the president has lost touch with key values. One administrative leader said of his president, "He gets into trouble with the faculty. He tries to go too fast. Faculty are traditional and departures must be discussed; he often doesn't allow adequate time for discussions to take place."

In this way, the path of the modal president leads to loss of faculty support, but continued support by the trustees and senior administrators.

The Path of the Failed Presidency

Failed presidencies begin like modal presidencies, but end with the president losing not only the confidence of the faculty, like the modal president, but also the confidence of the board or of administrative colleagues or even of both.

Authoritarian Leadership

Failed presidencies are created when presidents respond to a crisis by taking precipitate action without appropriate consultation, which is seen as violating faculty rights, or when their authoritarian leadership is not accompanied by conspicuous institutional success. Presidents are more likely to fail when the presidential selection process has not been considered legitimate.

Failed presidents see leadership as a process of downward influence, an attitude that is clearly apparent to the faculty. One ILP faculty leader described how his president acted, and the consequences for the faculty: "We met with the president to tell her what the faculty didn't like about what she was doing. She is more of a loner, she likes to be at the center, to be the boss. She doesn't give up power easily, even for a short duration. It's not always clear what her priorities are. . . . The faculty felt adrift and estranged. Things [were] going on without the faculty knowing about them. [There was a] need for communication between faculty and administration. When one analyzed the campus, it was clear that the president's leadership wasn't working. Her power base wasn't there."

The most common cause of a failed presidency is taking precipitate action without faculty consultation, usually early in the presidential career. It almost always involves the president engaging in a task-oriented, rational managerial act that appears insensitive to the human aspects of organization and misreads faculty culture. Faculty described one such situation by saying, "The president notified the faculty of the action but didn't negotiate or involve them. The president tried to appeal to the faculty, show them the problem, tell them it was essential that this be done, and show them the outcomes would be minimal." The president expected that the decision would be accepted by the faculty because it was a rational response to a serious institutional crisis. Instead, it was considered by them to be an outrageous violation of faculty status and rights.

Situations like this may sometimes lead to early presidential departure, but presidents who are indifferent to faculty views, and whose boards are unable or unwilling to intercede, can weather the immediate storm and continue a decade or longer in office. Whether presidents stay or leave, the incident remains fresh in the collective faculty mind, and years later is recited by faculty as a crucial turning point in the politics of the campus. One faculty member said of an old president's response to a long-ago crisis, "He acted in a manner contrary to faculty rights; his reaction to the situation ended his career." Another on a different campus said about an early presidential action seen as antifaculty, "He got off to a very bad start and never recovered. There is manifest distrust of him in the faculty. He simply does not understand the human reaction to this kind of thing." In some cases, presidents' actions leading to faculty disaffection were even initially supported by their boards or administrative colleagues because they appeared to reflect presidential competence, courage, or a "can-do" attitude.

Losing Nonfaculty Support

As a failed president's inability to work constructively with the faculty becomes evident, it eventually leads to loss of board or administration support as well. These normally loyal constituents come to see that presidential behaviors, ostensibly focused on institutional improvement, instead emphasize personal survival, self-justification, or self-aggrandizement. As one board leader finally came to realize, "The president believes he cannot be disagreed with. I feel the general welfare of the man is more important to him than the welfare of the institution he leads."

On the other hand, a few failed presidencies did not appear to have a precipitating event, but instead developed a downward trajectory through a steady erosion of confidence in a president who came to be seen as both authoritarian and incompetent. A president may be seen as authoritarian yet competent by faculty leaders when they believe that the campus has been conspicuously successful during the president's term. These presidents follow the modal path. But when the campuses of authoritarian presidents do not improve over time, trustees and other administrators may join the faculty in their expressions of dissatisfaction and add the charge of incompetence to the existing charge of authoritarianism.

Presidents whose selection process is seen as illegitimate by their faculties are at special risk for a failed presidency. They enter office without the expectation of success that provides a honeymoon for the modal president. While faculty expectations of presidential success provide more support for modal presidents than is objectively warranted during their early terms, the same principles operate negatively to lead faculty to be overly critical of presidents whose legitimacy is questioned, although this criticism may remain muted until it is provoked by a particularly grievous presidential action which the faculty see as contrary to their rights.

The Path of the Exemplary Presidency

Modal presidents, failed presidents, and exemplary presidents generally begin their terms supported by faculty, trustees, and administrators. Modal presidents lose faculty support, and failed presidents not only lose faculty support but also trustee and administrative support. Exemplary presidents maintain the support of the faculty throughout their institutional careers.

Maintaining Support

Exemplary presidents enter office with high faculty support, which they cultivate and preserve primarily by maintaining, even as they mature in office, the enthusiasm, institutional commitment, and desire to interact with faculty that typify new presidents. Exemplary presidents are seen as both competent and as sensitive to the social and political dynamics of their institutions. They not only make good decisions but follow good processes. The descriptions of two exemplary presidents by their faculty leaders reflect this combination of characteristics. Of one, it was said, "The president engenders and reinforces commitment from the people here. He walks around the college all the time, drops into faculty offices. He's caring. He takes a proprietary interest in this college. We don't agree on everything, but we agree to disagree." Of another, "He reads into the future and distills it for us and motivates us into action. He's very people oriented, knows everyone's name. He will remember what each of us is doing and our latest projects. He will often say the faculty is excellent. He is a strong person. He is a decisive decision maker."

Communication and Influence

The most important characteristic of exemplary presidents is that they are seen as continuing to respond to the faculty and willing to open themselves to faculty influence. They listen to faculty, and they support existing faculty governance mechanisms. While modal presidents are likely to treat communication and interaction as instrumental devices which become less important once they have learned about the campus, exemplary presidents are more likely to view them as essential and continuing components of evolving communities. The modal president sees communication as a means to an end; the exemplary president sees it as an end in itself.

Just as the dynamics that lead to modal or failed presidencies tend to be self-reinforcing, so too are the dynamics of exemplary presidencies. Because exemplary presidents identify faculty as the institution's strength, support faculty governance, and accept faculty influence, they tend to facilitate the development of responsible faculty leaders. In turn, these presidents then find that interaction with faculty is rewarding and helpful, and this supports their continued interaction.

The Development of Presidential Paths

New college presidents are faced with strong—and initially self-fulfilling—expectations that they will act to correct the deficiencies of their predecessors. They are likely initially to be judged as successful because their desire to learn and make sense of a new situation appears to demonstrate a high level of concern for constituent interests, their approach and focus of attention are seen as a welcome counterbalance to the behavior of the previous incumbent, and the succession crisis disturbs ongoing social systems and mutes criticism. Some new presidents are able to maintain the commitment and energy with which they began their tenure and, of greatest importance, remain accessible to faculty. They may become exemplary presidents. Other new presidents may ignore faculty and, early in their careers, take dramatic actions in the name of rationality that immediately cost them faculty support. They are likely to become failed presidents.

Most presidents follow a middle path. They begin their term with increased communication and high faculty support, which will gradually erode over time. As these new presidents gain experience, they find less need to rely on the perceptions of others to "make sense" of their college. They are more likely to depend on their own interpretations and judgments, less likely to solicit counsel, and therefore less likely to be seen as amenable to constituent influence. They come to act as if increased experience in leading reduces their dependence on others, when in fact the opposite may be true. At the same time, they have been unable to fulfill earlier expectations because, despite faculty perceptions, the campuses' problems were likely to have been created by external events rather than the shortcomings of the previous president, making the expectations unrealistic.

Even presidential behaviors initially applauded as correcting past deficiencies may become problematic in themselves if they continue when they are no longer appropriate. For example, a president may be brought in to strengthen academic affairs and correct a predecessor's emphasis on public relations. The president may be successful but then continue to focus on curriculum development, even as the institution moves into a new era requiring instead that the president engage in sophisticated legislative lobbying or strategic budget reallocating. Perceptions of presidential effectiveness diminish, and the cycle begins again.

Trustees, administrators, and faculty have different perceptions of presidential effectiveness, and it is possible for presidents to maintain trustee and administration support even as they become increasingly distant from the faculty. Presidents increasingly may rely on trustee and administration judgments to assess their own effectiveness. The common tendency to selectively seek information that supports their own position makes it possible for presidents to become even more certain of their positions as the quality of their decisions decreases (O'Reilly, 1990). Indications of faculty dissatisfaction may be rationalized, and insulated presidents may remain unaware of the extent of faculty concern.

College presidents enter their roles believing that they are effective institutional leaders. This belief is based on their previous accomplishments in positions of increasing institutional

status and confirmed by their selection as president over other
candidates in a competitive search process. It is reinforced by
the initial honeymoon period granted to new presidents. This
common beginning leads to three divergent paths, and whether
a presidency follow a modal, failed, or exemplary trajectory is
related to the characteristics of the president, the history of the
institution, the nature of the environment, and luck. Predicting the ultimate path of new presidents is fraught with difficulty,
since exemplary and modal presidents may look very much alike
as they begin their terms, and differences in faculty support become evident only over time. Failed and modal presidents, too,
may not look dissimilar initially, and their futures may be dif-
ferentiated as much by chance as by skill or temperament. Some
failed presidents make a fatal error early in their tenure when
faced with a difficult decision during a period of institutional
stress; other presidents have the good fortune of not being confronted with such a pivotal decision.

The three presidential paths are retrospective inventions
that can be ascribed with some degree of confidence only to presidents who have been in office for extended periods. Therefore,
we can look at the sixteen old ILP presidents in order to see
whether particular patterns of thinking and action can be associated with each path.

Presidential Paths, Thinking, and Behavior

Old presidents who followed the exemplary path were more likely
than the other two types to be cognitively complex and therefore able to interpret institutional life through multiple perspectives (Birnbaum, 1988a; Bensimon, 1989c). Three of the four
exemplary presidents, who had high faculty support, were seen
by constituents as highly complex; three of the five old presidents
with mixed faculty support were judged as reflecting medium
complexity, and six of the seven old presidents with low faculty
support were assessed as low in complexity.

Exemplary presidents are apparently less likely than others
to use linear strategy; indeed, none of the ILP exemplary presidents used linear strategy, while two of five presidents with mixed

support and five of seven presidents with low faculty support did. Exemplary presidents were also less likely than other presidents to use adaptive strategy (Neumann, 1989; Chaffee, 1984) and more likely to use interpretive strategy. They emphasized responsiveness to and interaction with faculty, and therefore viewed leadership as a process of social exchange based on reciprocity and mutual influence (Hollander, 1987). They shared authority through their support of governance systems and their respectful treatment of faculty leaders and expressed faculty will. They viewed their institutions as collective enterprises, and their concern with task was integrated with and inseparable from their concern for people and process. These presidents "took the role of faculty" (Bensimon, 1991b, p. 641), and were seen by the faculty as being like them and acting in a manner consistent with faculty views of reality. As a consequence, they had extraordinary influence in their organizations. One exemplary president said, "By sharing influence I have greatly increased my own influence. They know I'm willing to listen so they listen to me. I think the college is a political system. The president can't force others to do something, only persuade." The relationship between president and faculty was collaborative.

Old presidents identified as modal took a more linear view of influence sharing, seeing it as a means toward task achievement and a constraint to be overcome. They entered office believing that their ability to influence others depended on understanding the perceptions of reality held by constituents. But as they gained experience, the need for presidential sense-making decreased. They were likely to become increasingly focused on task accomplishment and give less attention to interacting with faculty before making decisions. Because presidents are usually quite capable, even their unilateral decisions can be objectively sound. This means that faculty may agree with the president's decisions, but remain uncommitted to them because they disapprove of the process through which they were made. Presidents who remove themselves from faculty influence can be seen by faculty as intelligent, logical, and competent, but still can be criticized for not giving sufficient attention to the human side of organizational life. A faculty leader commented unhappily about one such president: "He has difficulty in translating the concerns of the university so the faculty will understand them. He can't seem to function collegially. He is a military commander and we are his captains to whom he issues orders. He does not appreciate advice that is contrary to what he wants. He should not be president because [being president] is not only meetings and budgets and representing the university in the community, it also means being one [among] equals in the faculty."

This attitude, which may be particularly pervasive if the president is also seen as incompetent, may persist even if the institution is successful. As one disaffected faculty leader put it, "He has an irritating manner of being right, but it is the manner that irritates the faculty. We would get further if he were not so rough." Presidents often remain unaware that they have lost faculty support, because their interactions with supportive constituencies reinforce their views of their own effectiveness. Their interactions may eventually become self-sealing, preventing the presidents from hearing any disconfirming evidence and thus making presidential learning or change unlikely.

These data suggest that the loss of faculty support is not caused by a reduction of presidential mystique as constituents become more familiar with their presidents, but by a loss of confidence as decreasing interaction leads to more distance between them. For institutions with modal presidents, the relationship between president and faculty was competitive.

Failed presidents, even more than modal presidents, emphasized linear and directive orientations to leadership. When faced with a critical situation, they were likely to "take charge" and make unilateral decisions. These presidents were also more likely than others to see the faculty as the cause of institutional problems, and their solutions were likely to conflict with basic faculty values. For institutions with failed presidents, the relationship between president and faculty was adversarial.

Since institutions in this study were not selected through random sampling, these data cannot be used statistically to generalize to the universe of higher education. However, students of higher education may not find the following guesstimate based on the analysis of the sixteen old presidents in this study too implausible. The guesstimate says that by the time they leave office, approximately one-fourth of all incumbents will have followed the path of exemplary presidents; one-half, of modal presidents; and one-fourth, of failed presidents.

Do differences in presidential paths make a difference in college outcomes? Are exemplary presidents who view their colleges from multiple perspectives, listen carefully to constituents, remain open to influence, and emphasize interpretive strategy merely more likeable, or does their strong faculty support affect what presidents can hope to achieve?

Institutional Change and Exemplary Presidents

The four colleges with exemplary presidents were significantly different toward the end of the president's tenure than at the beginning. Each had undergone a change in mission such as a transition from single purpose to more comprehensive programs, a merger, or a dramatic shift in the relative emphasis given to teaching and research. Similar changes were evident in a number of institutions with modal or failed presidents, as well, but the campus responses were quite different.

At institutions without exemplary presidents, modifications in mission, program, enrollment, or funding were often seen as discontinuities with the past, and they frequently led to contention and conflict. Discussions over matters of substance were regularly bogged down in disagreements over governance and process. Presidential supporters and critics vied for influence, and disagreed over institutional purpose.

In contrast, changes at colleges with exemplary presidents were more likely to be seen either as constructive elaborations on historic themes or as reflections of a desirable new stage in institutional evolution. In either case, past and present were connected, and the president was identified as the link between them. These changes were celebrated rather than criticized and were a source of renewal, vitality, and enthusiasm that was recognized inside and outside the campus. One campus had started the 1980s with the mentality that it was a second-class institution. By the time of the first ILP visit, they saw themselves as in a period of rapid quality improvement and could say, "We are good, and heading to become the best." Several of the colleges that were only locally known at the beginning of the president's term later received statewide or national attention through a new program which drew visitors from across the country, publication of a study citing the high level of faculty morale, special recommendations in comparative college guides, or awards for programmatic excellence. This external acknowledgment of progress reinforced the colleges' self-confidence.

Each exemplary president was given major credit by constituents for the changes that had transpired. A faculty member at one campus that had experienced positive change said, "He has been able to accomplish so much in the years he has been here. He is responsible for the status and recognition the college has achieved in the community, the state, and I have to go a little further, in the nation." At another, a faculty leader said, "The college *is* the president. I can't think of anyone I'd rather have out there." At the same time, respondents on each campus identified other important campus leaders, and made it clear that the exemplary president, while perhaps necessary, was not a sufficient cause for campus improvement. In Chapter Six we will see how other individuals at a college also provide leadership.

CHAPTER 6

How Leadership
Is Shared

The two previous chapters have focused our attention on college presidents. Exemplary presidents led colleges that were extraordinarily successful. But to a lesser extent, many other colleges improved as well. How does a campus improve when its president is not well thought of?

Our culture has led people to ascribe leadership to persons in formally designated leadership roles, such as presidents. But it is often the case that the ideas, decisions, and behaviors of many campus participants come together to influence others and help shape a college's common perception of reality. Sometimes, this collective influence is generated by formal or informal institutional structures in which interaction is regularized and expected. At other times, it is a consequence of less patterned interactions that are infrequent, situational, or ad hoc. This chapter first summarizes information the ILP collected about the distribution of campus leadership and the reasons people are considered to be leaders. It then describes and illustrates how nonpresidential leadership can come from formal sources embedded in the institutional structure, as well as from informal sources that often emerge when individuals interact within the context of an institution's culture and history.

Who Are Campus Leaders?

People interviewed during the first ILP campus visit in 1986–87 were asked two deceptively simple questions. The first was, "Who do you think are some of the important leaders on this campus?" Interviewers provided no definition of "leader," leaving respondents to use whatever criteria they considered important. The second question, "Why do you consider them to be important leaders?" asked respondents in effect to explain and justify their nominations and, in doing so, to make manifest the implicit theories of leadership they held.

The responses of 170 persons who held five roles — board member, president, academic vice president, financial vice president, and faculty leader, were analyzed — first, to determine what role categories those viewed as leaders fell into, and second, to find out how often each category was named. Figure 1 shows the results for the thirteen different role categories which were named most frequently. The responses make it clear that leadership in academic institutions involves many figures and suggest a rich mosaic of interaction and influence that goes well beyond the simplistic notion that organizational functioning results from the actions of a single leader.

Presidents and Other Administrative Leaders

To find that there are a good number of leaders in every college is not to deny the importance of college presidents. On the contrary, presidents were named as campus leaders by 69 percent of the eligible respondents (presidents who named themselves were not counted). But although the president was the most frequently named leader, the academic vice president was seen as a leader by an almost equal number (65 percent). Deans were named by 44 percent of the respondents, with the importance of the role related to institutional type. Among universities, which were larger and more decentralized than other institutions, deans were mentioned as leaders more frequently than any other figure, including the president.

Figure 1. "Important Leaders on Campus," as Identified by Trustees, Presidents, Vice Presidents, and Faculty Leaders.

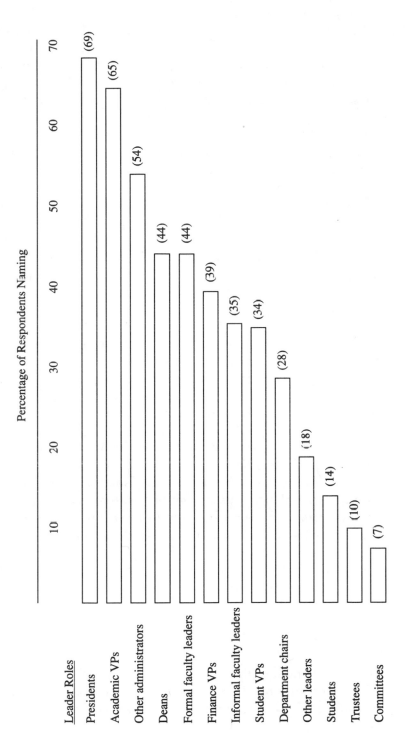

Percentage of Respondents Naming

Vice presidents for financial affairs and for student affairs were named as leaders by 39 and 34 percent, respectively, of those interviewed. Interestingly, vice presidents for student affairs were named by the president as frequently as other vice presidents, but much less so by other respondents. One president explained that "the vice president for student affairs would like to have more respect from the faculty; he has *my* ear, but he's not an opinion molder." The reason the vice president had the president's ear may have been captured by the respondent who referred to this vice president as "politically sensitive. His antennae are very acute. He is aware of people's attitudes about certain issues, changes. He is good at advising the president what to do. He knows what kinds of changes will throw this place into a tizzy."

More than half (54 percent) of all respondents identified as a leader at least one administrator who was not at the senior level. These "other administrators" were exceptionally diverse. On different campuses, they included directors of admissions, physical plant, enrollment management, intercollegiate athletics, research foundations, and learning resource centers, among others; opportunities for leadership were abundant throughout the administrative systems of many institutions. Though most people fill these roles in virtual obscurity, others rise to local prominence and visibility, perhaps owing to conspicuously successful performance or because of an institutional problem (for example in athletics), a shortage of resources, or the planning or development of a new building or program. Administrators were more likely than faculty to see leadership in these various administrative roles, perhaps because they had more opportunity than faculty did to work and interact with their administrative colleagues, or simply because, as administrators, they thought administration more important.

Faculty Leaders

It is not surprising that administrators, more visible because of their institutionwide responsibilities, were frequently named as leaders. It is more interesting that faculty were identified as leaders almost as often. Forty-four percent of the respondents listed as a leader one or more faculty members in formal leadership roles such as senate chair, union president, or head of an important committee. These professors engaged in quasi-administrative activities and were identified as leaders because of their perceived special competence. As an example, the chair of one faculty affairs committee was called an important leader because "he has ideas and sees them through. He doesn't just talk. He does his job. He comes up with new solutions that are unique and clever, not old. He persists, doesn't drop things, doesn't take forever to produce a document. He gets things done."

Thirty-five percent of the respondents also identified as leaders one or more faculty who were *not* at that time in any formal leadership position. Faculty without formal leadership roles were considered to be leaders for many reasons, but most commonly, because they had "good judgment, have been around long enough to be respected and recognized by the faculty; you can lean on them when you have a problem." They were also cited as leaders because they took their responsibilities seriously, were willing to do extra work and spend time, or were considered to be intellectual "heavyweights." But the most common reason was not what they did, but the respect with which others responded to them. As one faculty member said, "When they speak out everyone stops to listen. The positions they take are more likely to be adopted than anyone else's. At academic and faculty senate meetings, they are able to sway the membership. They carry a lot of respect in the college community.

Faculty could also be leaders because of their visibility in developing and championing new programs. As a consequence, one faculty leader said, "An academic leader can be anywhere in the professoriate — for example, dealing with a new program, a new course — and can dress it out to present it to the administration and can get it funded."

Department chairs were identified as leaders by a smaller proportion of respondents (28 percent). Just as administrators were more likely than faculty to see other administrators as leaders, faculty were more likely than administrators to see department chairs as leaders. The reasons they gave emphasized

both competence and the chair's representational role. One
faculty leader described a department chair as a leader by saying, "She is a remarkable administrator. She makes the faculty
feel their input is being considered. She speaks for how her
department feels. And all department chairs respect her. She
has the ability to engage you so you feel you have participated —
whether you have for real or not."

Other Leaders

At least three other definable roles or groups — board members,
students, and committees — were identified as leaders by small
numbers of respondents. Trustees were named as leaders by
10 percent of the respondents, and students by 14 percent. It
is a reflection of the unusual nature of academic institutions that
trustees — the constituency that is potentially most powerful by
virtue of the board's almost total legal authority — and students —
the constituency that is the most numerous — were seen relatively
infrequently as leaders. Even the small number of trustees who
were identified as leaders was misleadingly high, since it came
disproportionately from one campus with a still-active found-
ing trustee.

The smallest category of leaders, selected by 7 percent
of the respondents, consisted not of individuals but of groups
such as faculty senates, faculty unions, councils of deans, faculty
executive committees, alumni boards, or personnel and budget
committees. Although named infrequently, such groups reflect
the collegial nature of leadership in higher education and suggest that even those who may not be thought of as individual
leaders can exert leadership influence through their participation in important committees.

All roles not included in the previous twelve categories
were considered as "other leaders." The identification of these
other leaders was idiosyncratic to each campus, indicating that
the leadership structure of many institutions is in part a unique
function of personalities, history, and traditions. These leaders
filled such diverse roles as president's assistant or secretary, officer
of classified staff association, faculty member's spouse, alumni
president, or institutional lobbyist.

Why Are People Named as Important Leaders?

The concept of cognitive frames was introduced in Chapter Three as a way of describing institutional life from four vantage points — structural, collegial, political, and symbolic. When the reasons given for identifying a person or group as a leader are analyzed through the lenses of these same frames, it becomes clear that leaders not only fill different roles, but are seen as leaders for different reasons.

Structural Frame

A person using the structural frame would identify leaders for reasons such as their position in the hierarchy, involvement in decision making, technical or professional competence, or perceived exercise of power. Almost half (47 percent) of those identifying a leader mentioned elements of the structural frame, making this the most common frame in use. Presidents and provosts in particular were seen as leaders because "they have the power; they make the decisions." Similarly, other senior administrators were identified as leaders because they had been delegated authority by the president. While most respondents identified individual roles, some used the structural frame to generalize across the entire institution. As one board member said when asked to identify leaders, "If you just take the administrative chart and go down from there, you will see who the leaders are."

Political Frame

The second most common frame, used in 26 percent of the leader depictions, was political. In this mode, people were identified as leaders because they helped acquire resources, influenced others, "made things happen," were open to influence, shared power, or were seen as representatives of important campus groups. Presidents were viewed from this perspective less often than others (19 percent), while faculty members without formal leadership roles were depicted in these terms relatively often (36 percent). An academic vice president was seen through the political frame, for example, because he had "access to the key faculty leadership. He is the president's interface with the faculty. He represents the president to the faculty senate. He has the pulse of the faculty. If a faculty member complains, [that faculty member] goes to him first."

Students and faculty were sometimes identified as leaders because they were seen as representing and influencing important constituencies such as specific faculty groups, ethnic groups, student groups, or women's groups. For example, a faculty union officer was identified as a leader because "he and other union people are in touch with more of the constituency on a constant basis than anyone else on campus. As such, they have more insight, people go to them to speak about everything and anything."

Collegial Frame

Individuals qualified as leaders through the collegial or human relations frame because they were team players, fair, encouraged others to participate in institutional life, had "the personal touch," or led by example. They were seen as considerate, relaxed, or able to defuse tense situations with humor. This frame was only the third most common of the four in use, characterizing just 14 percent of the responses, and was employed approximately equally in the various leadership roles. An administrator thus described was seen as "competent, articulate, kind, a people person. He is a maintenance kind of administrator; he keeps morale high. He keeps people happy. He is a nice person. He gets his assignments done well."

Symbolic Frame

The frame least frequently mentioned was the symbolic. It accounted for 13 percent of the responses, identifying people or groups as leaders because they appeared to embody the institution's purpose or reflect its values, or because of their vision, large perspective, and visibility. A president seen through this lens was defined by one constituent as "a symbol of the institution and its stability. He is a Statue of Liberty type of person—he embodies what America is." A faculty leader described another president in symbolic terms by saying:

On campus, he establishes himself as the symbol
of leadership. If the faculty have an idea, he will
trumpet it, and if people say yes to it, he will find
the money to make ideas happen. He is visionary.
He is in a supportive role. He wants to bring good
ideas to the campus and he takes good ideas from
it. I am into perception. It is essential. It is like
Ronald Reagan. The reason people like him is because he cares about America. Well, we can say
about the president that he cares about the college.
If you can get people to believe this, they will do
whatever they can for you.

Formal Sources of Leadership

The most obvious formal source of leadership at many institutions was the president, but the data already presented indicate
that several other formal sources often exist as well. Two examples, one from the administrative sector and one from the
faculty, will provide a better sense of the way they function as
leaders.

The Academic Vice President

On many campuses, the academic vice president (AVP) had
as great — or even greater — effect on the campus than did the
president. As one faculty leader said, "For most faculty, the
leader isn't the president, it's the AVP. There is much curiosity
about what the president does. The AVP is at the heart of initiatives, wheeling and dealing with the board and on campus."
The leadership role of the AVP may be particularly important
for reasons which are as much structural as personal; while a
president's major activities may involve external representation
and fund-raising, the AVP is more often engaged in the day-
to-day activities that directly influence the lives of faculty and
administrators.

At one ILP institution, for example, a major reason cited
by faculty for institutional improvement was the appointment
of a new academic vice president. He spent his first months on

campus visiting in the offices of department chairs, listening to discussions of academic issues, and touring the campus, in addition to reading reports and studies. A faculty leader said, "He was a quick study. He learned an enormous amount about the college — I mean the subtext, where the pressure points are, the tensions. Some of these things were very big items. In an astonishingly short time he came to meetings of the administrative council and the faculty senate with a plan to fix some of the serious problems of the institution, which were in the academic organization." The vice president was able to work with faculty leaders to develop a major academic reorganization plan that was strongly endorsed by the senate and was credited with being a primary determinant of a new sense of motion on the campus. As one campus observer said, "Now that we have the new vice president, the institution is primed to go. I am much more optimistic for change. People are participating, following. They are a big catalyst in the process. The institution is finally pulling together." The influence of the vice president was ascribed to his expertise and strong academic background, openness, patience, lack of self-aggrandizement, skills in working with people, and ability to function within established governance processes. He was known as a good listener and as someone who asked good questions. He expressed concern for finding ways to pull the faculty together as they confronted important institutional issues.

While an AVP can have a major effect on a campus, that effect was not always seen by constituents as positive. At one institution, the AVP was unable to collaborate with the faculty, and instead seemed at war with them. The faculty had not been involved in the selection process, and the AVP was viewed as having contempt for faculty governance. The AVP acknowledged being primarily concerned with tasks and spending little time attending to the interpersonal dimensions of the position. The vice president interpreted faculty antipathy as further justification for the need to make decisions without consultation and incorrectly assumed that a take-charge style led to being seen by others as an effective administrator: "I have not found it easy to delegate and have something done. I find I have to intervene or do it over again. I find I have to sort out a lot of detail for things to get done. I have found it just takes some time and effort to organize things. And that is why I am where I am, because people recognize that I am good at that and this place needs it." At that institution, faculty withdrew from program development activities and marked time in the hope that new leadership would emerge.

Senates and Unions

The normative relationship between administration and faculty in a college is considered to be one of shared authority. On most campuses, the collective authority of the faculty at the institutional level is manifested through a senate, a union, or both. Shared authority implies shared leadership, and since both senates and unions are formal structures, the heads of these organizations at least by title fill leadership roles. But whether senates and unions at ILP institutions actually provided leadership is another matter. While both senates and unions had the potential for real leadership, certain factors could inhibit the realization of that leadership potential on many campuses.

In her multiple case study of governance systems at three ILP institutions, Lee (1991) concluded that three related factors contributed to the perceived effectiveness of a faculty senate: structure, the cultural context in which the governance system operated, and the interaction between the faculty governance structure and the administration. Lee described institutions with relatively effective and ineffective senates and identified ways in which senates and unions worked together.

An Effective Senate. One institution's effective senate had been established with administration support and encouragement from the president. Informants repeatedly mentioned that the administration completely respected the senate's scope of authority. The provost met regularly with the senate executive committee, the senate chair was a member of the president's cabinet, and communication between those in faculty and administrative leadership roles was frequent and informal. Administrative deference to the senate's role was high and consistent, and the administration would not permit "end runs" around the senate structure. The administration had rejected only one senate recommendation in recent years. This administration support of the senate was pragmatic, rather than ideological. One administrator said, "The ability to effect change is difficult in a mature organization with very powerful faculty. It takes patience if you want the faculty to come along with you. I would rather take longer and have the faculty on board than push something through."

There were still complaints about the senate—some said it did not select the strongest faculty for leadership roles, the structure was too complex, and it acted too slowly. But the campus consensus was that the relationship between the senate and the administration was crucial to the institution's efforts to improve quality.

A Paralyzed Senate. In contrast, another institution found its senate system paralyzed. A history of patriarchal presidents and captive senates made it impossible for the senate to function effectively even as a new president invited faculty participation. Administrators continued to criticize the senate and those in senate leadership roles for ineffectiveness, overlooking the roots of that behavior in previous administrative actions. Lee pointed out that "all parties are so busy pointing fingers at each other that little constructive effort is being made to resolve the situation. Particularly when the system is stressed by external pressures for change, the energy devoted to blaming drains the ability to focus on how that change will occur" (1991, p. 53). The president in this situation chose, probably not atypically, to work around the senate rather than to try to heal it. At the same time, while the administration was exhorting the senate to exercise more leadership, it was sending the message that the institution's problems were the faculty's fault.

Senates and Unions. Much the same processes, problems, and opportunities seen in the relationships between administrators and senates applied also to faculty unions. When there was a history of constructive relationships and a recognition and respect of the role of the other group, unions could make important contributions to institutional development. Where there was a history of disruptive conflict and lack of respect, the union became a force to maintain the status quo, limit administrative discretion, and continually fuel the fire of discord and mistrust.

Leadership from Individuals and Informal Groups

Although people are most likely to identify leadership through the structural frame, institutional life is constantly influenced by people and groups acting outside of the formal campus hierarchy. ILP researchers identified a good number of further examples of individual faculty members and administrators — some in leadership roles and others not — who engaged in acts of leadership with consequences for a campus. These acts could involve something as simple as asking a question or as complex as starting a new program.

- An informal faculty group visited the president to tell him they had lost confidence because of his handling of fiscal matters. The president sounded out some additional faculty members the next day and then immediately resigned. The trustees later expressed appreciation to the faculty for taking an action that they knew to be in the college's interest.
- The vice presidents of a college in crisis banded together and told the trustees that the board's plan to fill the recent presidential vacancy with an old retired trustee was unacceptable. The board reconsidered and instead selected a president from the existing administrative staff.
- An executive assistant pointed out that a videotape being developed for recruitment purposes used classroom scenes dominated by white men, and this action changed the way the videotape producers thought about the materials they were producing and the image of the college they were portraying.
- After several years of informal and inconclusive senate discussion, a faculty leader boldly asked the institutional president to name faculty members to senior administrative com-

mittees. The president immediately agreed. When asked later why he had not named faculty to these committees earlier, the president replied that no one had ever asked him before. The faculty leader had changed the president's perceptions of appropriate governance structures.

- The new vice president for student affairs got students involved in planning Founder's Day celebrations, and turned what one faculty leader described as "a dismal and structured affair . . . something to be avoided" into "a riotous celebration" that changed people's perceptions of the nature of their community.

- A faculty member did surveys and studies, brought in consultants, and initiated a student retention program with intensive faculty participation at a campus at which there had been no administrative initiatives dealing with education or institutional quality. Her activities changed the perceptions of others from resigned acceptance of student weaknesses to an enthusiastic understanding of how faculty could make a difference in student performance.

- A faculty member took over as chair of the campus committee on general education after the senate had rejected the committee's newly developed general education program. By conducting hearings, visiting departments, building consensus, and changing people's perceptions about faculty responsibility for curricular coherence, he succeeded in getting approval where the formal administrative and faculty governance structure had failed.

Each of these can be seen as incidents of leadership because they changed the ways in which others on campus constructed their sense of reality.

Implications of Dispersed Leadership

On every campus there are persons other than the president who are seen by others as providing leadership. Often these people are themselves in formal leadership roles, such as vice presidents, deans, or heads of important faculty groups. But people with no formal leadership roles provide leadership as well.

Giving attention to the complex dynamics of organizational leadership, instead of focusing on the myth of heroic presidential leadership, emphasizes that leadership involves interdependencies between roles and that roles change over time. The differentiation between leader and follower thus becomes increasingly arbitrary.

Leaders cannot succeed without followers. In higher education, these "followers," often faculty, are usually articulate, enthusiastic, and intelligent people whose training, socialization, and disposition leads them to believe in the importance of

THE FAR SIDE   By GARY LARSON

"Well, what d'ya know! . . . *I'm* a follower, too!"

what their institution does. They exemplify the idea that effective followers are not people who merely follow orders passively or uncritically. Rather, good followers "think for themselves and carry out their duties and assignments with energy and assertiveness. . . . They are risk takers, self-starters, and independent problem solvers" (Kelley, 1988, pp. 143–144). In fact, good followers are much like good leaders, and in higher education, people who fill a leadership role in one setting often find themselves to be followers in another. The faculty chair who influences perceptions of appropriate promotions criteria at Tuesday's college faculty personnel committee may be distributing the dean's handouts at Friday's faculty meeting.

Formal leaders can make a difference, but institutions can improve without them, or despite them, if they have effective followers. Effective followers take initiative, are committed to the institution's purposes, see themselves as the equals of leaders, have high performance standards, and search for overlooked problems. Those in leadership roles can facilitate or hinder the effectiveness of follower initiative; they cannot demand it. Much of what happens in a college is due to the effectiveness of people in follower roles who, without title or authority, take initiative to do what they believe has to be done. As the number of such persons increases in a college, leadership becomes more dispersed. The college becomes a cauldron of ideas and interaction. Groups without "leaders" can be productive, because their members themselves have the qualities of effective leadership. Followers share leadership tasks when they behave responsibly respecting the institution's purposes. Good leaders empower followers to share the burdens of leadership, and in exchange good constituents produce good leaders (Gardner, 1990).

A consideration of the large number of different leaders seen by various campus constituents serves as a useful corrective to the idea that all leadership in academic organizations comes from the top. Had more people been interviewed, including those not among the leadership elite, an even larger and more diverse listing of leaders would have emerged. The responses of constituents provide some important clues about this diversity of leadership in the academic environment.

Clearly, no one on campus — not even the president — is likely to be seen as a leader by everyone; although 69 percent of the ILP respondents identified their president as an important campus leader, the president was *not* named by 31 percent. Discussions about academic leadership that focus exclusively on the president or other senior administrators, and even those that are expanded to include formal leadership roles in other constituency groups, thus oversimplify the reality of most institutions.

At the same time, people are more likely to be thought of as leaders if they occupy positions in the campus hierarchy. These positions give them visibility and salience and require them to do things, such as make decisions, that are consistent with our culture's view of what leaders ought to do. The mere fact of their visibility leads people to identify them as leaders by association. People are therefore more likely to be thought of as leaders if they are either highly visible (such as the president) or if they interact frequently with the person making the judgment. Vice presidents for student affairs, for example, are more likely to be identified as leaders by their presidents, who see them in staff meetings and who rely on them to provide a sense of campus mood, than by faculty to whom they are virtually invisible. Department chairs are called leaders by faculty, who see them regularly and know the tasks they perform, but not by financial vice presidents who seldom meet them. This means that people seen as followers by some may be seen as leaders by others.

The ILP findings suggest two further points. One is that many of the same characteristics are identified whether people talk about presidents, vice presidents, faculty, or others: good leaders are seen as good listeners, responsive to others, competent, and committed to the institution and integrated into its culture.

Finally, perceptions and assessments of leadership are embedded in values. Talking in terms of roles and changing others' views of reality ignores the questions of leadership for whom and leadership for what ends. Particularly in discussing leaders and leadership of constituency groups such as senates and unions, the absence of a value dimension becomes trouble-

some. We have seen, for example, how a senate chair can per-
petuate a climate of distrust so that the senate becomes a sentry
to protect against the forays of an administration believed to
wish to weaken the faculty's role; people are then chosen for
leadership roles based on their avowed willingness to reject administrative influence. The administration, in turn, increasingly
believes the senate leadership is not representing the best of the
faculty, which enables the administration to discount the senate's
legitimacy. The actions of each influence the other, even if not
in ways that they intend. They each respond to a different constituency and attempt to alter what that constituency does or
how it interprets campus events. The college president and the
senate head may each be filling a leadership role and exercising
leadership. And yet the outcomes for the campus may not be
progress and development, but stagnation and conflict. Both
leaders are doing what they think is best, given the environment in which they find themselves, and from their different
perspectives, both see that environment as a "given" rather than
as an enacted reality that they themselves have in good measure created.

It is discomforting to be including influence of this sort
as an example of leadership, and yet it is leadership by definition. Is it good leadership? The answer depends on the eyes of
the beholder. Still, dilemmas like this suggest the problems of
looking at leadership from the perspective of a single interest.
A good leader, whether president, dean, or senate chair, should
be recognized as effective by many campus constituencies, not
just one. People usually achieve that recognition when they are
seen, not merely as protecting narrow interests of one group,
but as integrating their group's needs into a larger understanding of institutional purpose. Leadership is not a zero-sum game,
but a process of reciprocal influence in which power increases
as it is shared. Good leaders beget more good leaders.

Dispersed leadership may weaken an institution when constituents are at war, but it typically strengthens an institution
when there are accepted forums within which various leaders
can constructively interact. The realities of presidents and their
constituents often differ, so that the good faith efforts of one

group to improve their college may be inconsistent with the interests of another. Such differences are normal and expected in a complex and uncertain world, and they are usually resolved on campus through long-standing structural, collegial, and political processes. When these processes are widely accepted as legitimate, they facilitate exchanges among various groups and individuals. Presidents are important participants in these transactions, but ordinarily cannot get their own way much of the time. When these transactions take place within a healthy governance system, the usual outcome is incremental institutional change and improvement.

Occasionally, however, some presidents are able to exert extraordinary influence on their institutions. These presidents help constituents move toward greater agreement about what is real and what is important, so their activities and commitments become mutually reinforcing rather than conflicting. When this occurs, the consequence can be institutional renewal. In Chapter Seven, we will define renewal and examine how it was brought into being on two very different college campuses.

CHAPTER 7

Leadership
and Campus Renewal

We have seen that leadership is dispersed at academic institutions and that presidents share influence with other college leaders. The existence of multiple sources of leadership meant that institutions could improve even when their presidents were not considered particularly effective. At some ILP colleges, leaders competed with each other, so that gains in one facet of functioning might come at the expense of losses in another. But on campuses with exemplary presidents, leaders shared values and commitments and worked collaboratively.

Institutional renewal was associated with collaborative leadership. Colleges exist to enrich individual lives, promote the search for knowledge, and assist the human quest to achieve a civil and just social community. People work in these institutions because they too cherish those same purposes, and regard their colleges as vehicles through which they can serve society and put their own values into action. But organizational life is fraught with ambiguities and harsh realities. All too frequently, even people with high ideals, trying to cope with the seemingly intractable problems of day-to-day life, lose sight of ends and get caught up in means. To renew a college is to help its participants reaffirm their values, replenish their energy and commitment, find satisfaction in their collective enterprise, and share the belief that their present success is a precursor to even higher achievement in the future. College presidents can play a key role in the renewal process.

Leadership leading to renewal was not the norm among ILP institutions. It was apparent at four colleges, all of which had old presidents who were rated as exemplary. Renewal also appeared to be in progress at several institutions with new presidents, although it is more difficult to make such judgments in the early stages of a president's career. The difficulty is compounded by the renewing effect of the succession cycle itself; campuses expect to experience renewal under an incoming president, and new presidents' behavior usually encourages that view.

To begin to understand the phenomenon of renewal, we can look at an analysis and comparison of the presidents and circumstances of two ILP institutions that experienced renewal. We will call them State College and Research College. State College was headed by an old president whom the ILP identified as exemplary. Research College was led by a new president whose path could also become clearly exemplary if it continues its present course. Both colleges had developed programs that enhanced and confirmed core institutional values, generated excitement and commitment, and enhanced the performance of the entire institution. In both cases, presidents who enjoyed strong faculty support played critical roles.

This chapter describes the ways in which these two presidents worked with other campus leaders — particularly faculty leaders — to renew their colleges. Because the institutions, their presidential leaders, and the programs they developed were so different, the common threads which ran through the experiences of the two campuses deserve attention, for they may serve to illustrate and illuminate those aspects of presidential leadership that may make a positive difference.

State College

Anyone familiar with comprehensive public institutions would immediately feel comfortable on the campus of State College. Its moderately sized urban campus is attractive, but not plush. Its buildings, a mixture of State College Modern and State College Traditional, are functional without frills. Its faculty is unionized, and its commuting student body is unselective (that is, performing at an average high school level) and ethnically diverse.

State College's funding per student was among the lowest in its state system, and its operations were subject to many state-imposed restrictions. Trustees, administrators, and faculty alike articulated their belief in the values of diversity and opportunity, and identified the goal of the campus as increasing quality without limiting access. The president called it "a college of opportunity. We are not a highly selective school. Here a very diverse population gets to rise to their level of capacity. The quality of our institution is determined by what we do for our students." College leaders pointed with pride to the contrast between the limited horizons suggested by the low SAT scores of entering freshmen and the significant employment opportunities open to them after graduation.

The program responsible for renewing State College was funded by a large external grant, secured competitively. The grant proposal had several integrated components which included attention to student access and persistence, strengthening of general education, and expanding faculty and staff development. But its centerpiece was the design and implementation of a value-added student assessment program in which all academic departments were to participate.

After three years of operation, the program was considered highly successful by all segments of the campus community. The president believed that it had a "profound impact; the campus is very different now academically," and a faculty leader said, "Our campus right now is more successful than it has ever been." Another college leader said, "Our quality is improving. We have higher retention, more diversity; our graduates are more satisfied and doing better. There is a strong will on this campus to improve the quality of instruction." Yet another commented on "massive changes by faculty in attention to their teaching."

The progress noted by those inside the institution was confirmed by an external team of observers (unrelated to the ILP), which had followed the program from its inception. The observers reported that the program had succeeded brilliantly. Faculty who were originally reluctant to participate were now enthusiastic and had taken ownership of the program. They saw assessment not only as a tool for measuring learning but as a vehicle for improving instruction. Campus diversity had also significantly increased.

Prior to the development of the assessment program, State College was a successful but average institution of its kind. Subsequently, it became a vibrant, energetic, and committed community. This community had found a way to work together, through which it could finally clarify and implement the college's oft-stated goals of excellence and equity. The college had been renewed.

The President

The president of State College had been in office for close to two decades. He was a "local" who had earned his undergraduate and graduate degrees in institutions within a fifty-mile radius of the college. He had been a faculty member and department chair at the college before assuming the presidency. At the time of his appointment, he was well known to all institutional constituencies and enjoyed strong support.

The president thought of himself as first among equals, and through his informal manner, attempted to diminish hierarchical differences on campus. He described the institution as a political system: a "pluralistic democracy," with himself as a "governor." Presidential influence was manifest through education and coalition building, and the president saw his power as the ability to persuade. He said, "I do this by going to people and talking to them. I drop ideas to them and they pick them up. And I know whom to drop the ideas to. I have never had a major program that we wanted that I have not been able to get through."

Although the president met regularly with his senior staff and with faculty groups, the president was not constrained by the college's structure, and much college business was conducted informally. Administrative subordinates and faculty were as likely to drop by the president's office, or meet in small groups at his home, as he was to stop by theirs.

The president advised new presidents to learn about their campuses by "getting out, and get to know people as fast as you

can. Get to know their needs, and let them know what you want
to do. Go to individuals' offices. Spend a lot of time doing this.
Meet people on their own ground." After close to two decades
in office, he was still following his own advice. He would frequently be seen here and there on campus and regularly attended
campus social functions. College leaders agreed that his practice of management by walking around and his approachable
and informal style provided him with a constant flow of information. He was committed to open communication and sensitive to feedback; he described himself as having firm values and
principles, but willing to change the methods through which he
would try to implement them.

     He was considered by others as a strong leader as well
as "the first of the teaching faculty." He saw his major interests
as curriculum and education, and identified himself as "the
educational leader of the college." He had come from the faculty,
and others said about him that "the college is his life." And, indeed, the president was seldom away from the campus and was
seen as being knowledgeable about everything important going on.

Other Sources of Leadership

At State College, the acknowledged leadership of the president
in developing the idea of assessment was complemented by the
leadership of the faculty and, in particular, the faculty union.
One administrative leader said, "This place is a cauldron. Lots
of things are going on all the time. There's little faculty resistance
here. Faculty feel confidence in their faculty leaders. The important element is interaction between the president and the
union leaders. It's because of shared governance — the union and
the senate and administration working together." And a union
member added, "If you look at the development of the college,
virtually everything is a result of the union's ability to work collectively with the administration." Faculty had great faith in their
union leadership, and were likely to engage in activities that
carried the union's blessing. Programs seen as being developed
jointly by the union and administration were likely to be ac-

cepted; programs that were not developed cooperatively were likely to be rejected by the faculty. A union leader commented, "Things move very fast around here because we talk to each other on so many matters. The strength of the union here is caused by the strength of the administration. The influence pie grows."

The board of trustees at State College endorsed the assessment program, but the board was seen more as a campus watchdog than as a campus defender. The president enjoyed strong board support early in the development of the assessment project, at the time of the first campus visit. At the time of the second visit, some trustees were thought to believe that close union-administration relationships were inappropriate, and they were critical of the president's failure to "stand up to" the union and keep it at arm's length. Board members acknowledged and defended instances of trustee intrusion and micromanagement.

Relationships at State College were characterized by a strong and stable administration, a strong and stable union, and most important, constant and nonadversarial communications between them. The union could operate nondefensively because the president invariably treated its leaders as colleagues, kept them fully involved, and did not try to subvert them by going outside established communication channels.

Managing Renewal

At State College, administrative and faculty leaders met with each other frequently and informally. Joint committees were the norm, and consultation was the expected order of the day. The first step in developing the proposal for the assessment program was a retreat to generate ideas, in which large numbers of faculty and administrative leaders participated; this was followed by the formation of a large campuswide task force representing different campus constituencies. The faculty union was considered integral to the decision-making processes of the institution and was an active participant in all major college decisions. Both the union and the president credited this relationship as essential to the development of the assessment program.

An administrator said, "If these things were happening top-down, it would not work, because faculty would suspect that assessment was being used to judge them. Here the faculty played the major role in developing the assessment program." The continual communication meant that "things move very fast around here because we talk to each other so frequently on so many matters." It also meant that directive approaches were not acceptable; as one leader said, referring to a U.S. efficiency engineer of the early 1900s, Frederick W. Taylor, "you can't employ Tayloristic, top-down, rationalistic approaches. People have to be induced." At State College, the emphasis was not on data but on the politics of moving toward consensus and getting people to participate. According to one administrator, the campus had developed "ratios and stuff—student/faculty, class size—but no one was interested in them. Data are available but are not used because they always run up against resistance."

Administrators and faculty (including union) leadership were involved at all stages of the assessment program and participated in decisions about its structure and policies, as well as its operational details. The most sensitive aspect of the program—developing the policies and guidelines for the assessments of departments—was made the responsibility of the faculty senate. The campus culture reinforced the idea that campus initiatives should be constructed to minimize any possibility that they might be seen as coercive or punitive. The assessment program at State College was therefore designed to be separate from other institutional systems and processes, and its outcomes could not be used to make comparisons between programs or departments or to evaluate individual faculty.

As a consequence, assessments were neither integrated into the college's program review and accreditation process nor connected to the college's academic hierarchy. Deans were "outside the [assessment] loop." The separation was consistent with the program's avowed purpose of permitting individual departments to change. One administrator said, "We don't look at assessment as an accountability mechanism, but as a learning tool. We're helping faculty to improve." The advantage of this separation was that faculty "bought in" to the process and freely participated. The disadvantages were that program administration and evaluation were believed to be less effective than they could be, and deans who had responsibility for program review did not have access to assessment data that could have provided great insight into their programs.

Although coordinated from above by faculty-dominated committees, assessment was highly decentralized and localized in operation. The faculty of each department of instruction developed the procedures through which it refined its goals and objectives, created an assessment plan, implemented pilot tests, and planned improvements. The purpose was to permit faculty to understand the relationship between their goals and student outcomes, and to revise curricula as appropriate. There was no preconceived structure for the assessment, and the programs varied greatly between academic units. While this might have reduced efficiency, the college believed that "if you tried to monitor closely, you would create resistance. You have to proceed in a temperate, modest way. This is a college, not a factory."

Institutional Values

Teaching and student support were almost universally the major themes running throughout the interviews with administrators and faculty. One administrative leader commented that State College "takes great pains to be personal and close in serving its students and in building rapport among faculty and staff. There is a family feeling here."

The culture of State College endorsed principles of access, support for underprepared students, and social justice. The president defined his own value system as based on "social democracy, so I home in on issues of diversity and on programs for people who need to make a living. The traditional notions of quality and reputation have to be challenged. We have to take our students where they come from." The president's self-identification as a "populist" was complemented by the egalitarian ethic of unionism. One union leader said, "I was attracted to State College because of the wide student access it permits—

the open enrollment. These are the values of the president, the union, and the faculty senate; that is the institution's commitment." The commitment to opportunity was lived as well as espoused. The college had been offered an opportunity by the state to increase its per-student financial support if it would reduce enrollments by raising admissions standards. The college called this elitist and refused, an action recalled with pride by faculty, trustees, and administrators alike.

Those aspects of the renewal program that emphasized minority student enrollment and retention were clearly consistent with the values the college placed on equity and access. The assessment program was consistent with other campus and professional values as well. The stated goal was program improvement and student satisfaction, both major elements in the college's culture of teaching and individual development. Materials collected as part of the program could not be used for any other purpose, such as faculty assessment. While this separation had costs, it was consistent with both the college's teaching values and its desire to foster a protective environment for colleagues. In addition, the group processes through which the program was initially developed, the ability of each department to design its own program, and the review of department activities by a campuswide peer group committee all supported the college's collegial and collaborative orientations. The president was seen as "making decisions that are consistent with the mission, goals, and objectives, but he also takes initiatives as a situation permits."

Research College

Research College is a prestigious private institution that gives attention both to its diverse undergraduate curriculums and to its highly regarded programs of research and graduate training. Its expansive campus, made up of both modern structures and buildings of handsome traditional stone, suggests an environment in which both cutting-edge scholarship and close student-faculty relationships might flourish. Half of its undergraduates rank in the top 5 percent of their high school class, and almost all reside on campus. Its endowment, grant, and tuition income place it among the top colleges in the nation.

Trustees, administrators, and faculty at Research College emphasized the development of institutional quality as defined by meritocratic criteria. They were particularly proud of the accomplishment of their graduates in business and the professions and the acknowledged excellence of many of their graduate programs. The goals of the campus were to become even more attractive to the strongest undergraduate and graduate students, to increase research support, and to move up in national ratings based on reputation.

Research College assessed itself on the basis of improvement in the quality of its scholarship and increased levels of grants and publications. The program responsible for renewing Research College emphasized a comprehensive and centrally coordinated system of academic planning and program review. Campus leaders described it as a process through which the institution could raise the quality of every academic unit, while reallocating resources to achieve overall distinction and eminence in selected areas. The program at Research College was predicated on the reallocation of the base budget and required no additional funding.

At Research College, the new processes for planning and allocating resources were widely praised and were believed to have been responsible for redefining the programs of many departments, revising some curriculums, increasing interunit cooperation, and creating strategies for more external funding. Budgets were balanced, enrollments were up, and enthusiasm was high. One administrator said, "We have gone from a laissez-faire, carefree system to one of reality," and another commented that the program had permitted the institution to make selective investments and to "level up." The new openness and discipline brought to the planning process had made decisions more acceptable. An administrator pointed out that "in the past, no one knew why certain programs were given priority, or how things got to be on the agenda. The process of identifying priorities is now more satisfying to people."

Prior to the implementation of its planning and program review process, Research College was a well regarded, prestigious institution that many believed had not fully achieved its potential. Some characterized it as poorly managed and academically complacent and unfocused. Subsequently, participants were able to see that they were no longer drifting in place but making substantial progress toward improving their programs and the institution's stature. A sense of lost opportunity had been replaced by excitement and a belief that their goal of being judged to be one of the handful of premier institutions in the United States was not only desirable, but achievable. The college had been renewed.

The President

The president of Research College was a recent appointment. He was a cosmopolitan who had served as a faculty member and administrator in other institutions, some of which were of equal or greater prestige than the one he now headed. The president placed considerable emphasis on creating rationalized management structures and processes. His most immediate actions on taking office were to learn the budget, spend time with the deans, and develop a planning process. He described himself as directly involved in the affairs of the institution, as a "hands-on" manager for those who liked what he did, and a "meddler" for those who didn't.

In addition to overseeing the planning and program evaluation process, he spent considerable time in reviewing management procedures, with particular emphasis on the budget. At the same time, he was politically astute and highly sensitive to the limits of his authority. He recognized that leadership in higher education has "a subtle meaning because it encompasses persuasion and consensus building." The president was aggressive in seeking information, placed considerable reliance on formal reporting systems, and tried to integrate information collection into formal managerial processes. At the same time, he too practiced management by walking around, and he described his tours of the campus, forums with students, breakfasts, and other informal activities.

The president was seen by other administrative leaders as a strong leader and a "tough" manager with a highly developed sense of academic quality. He was also thought of as open and accessible. His style was seen as one that "invited participation rather than being dictatorial," although it was widely believed that once he had made up his mind he was unlikely to change it.

Unlike many cosmopolitan presidents, he was seen as minimizing off-campus activities. He was interested in management as a means to improving education and not as an end in itself. The president saw his position in a private institution as an opportunity to work on educational quality, in preference to serving as an "underpaid lobbyist or chief clerk" as the president of an institution in the public sector.

Other Sources of Leadership

At Research College, faculty leadership had stagnated under the previous administration, which was seen as not taking faculty governance seriously. That changed significantly as the new president actively sought consultation. As a result, more senior faculty members had begun to participate in governance, and faculty were becoming more influential in institutional affairs. The president was seen as providing directive leadership, which was accepted by the faculty and consistent with the values and traditions of the campus. One administrator said, "Faculty here collectively prefer to have leadership come from above if the leader can establish credibility. There is an unusually smooth working relationship here — a reflection of institutional well-being. The faculty are willing to cede decision making because of the president's success."

The board of trustees was composed of prestigious community leaders, professionals, and business people, and it strongly supported the president. The board was not involved in institutional management, but the board members recognized the leadership of the president because, as one trustee said, "Most are CEOs and they know [leadership] when they see it." The board saw itself as "more supporting the president than initiating action. It is helping him to get the resources to get the job done."

Relationships at Research College were described by administrators and faculty alike as reflecting a climate of mutual respect and civility. One administrator said, "There is a sense of reasonableness. Faculty really want to make this a better place." Policy initiatives were likely to come from administrators, and to be elaborated through administrative interaction. However, this took place in an environment in which opportunities for communication and influence were widely available. A faculty leader noted that regular meetings took place between the faculty executive committee and the senior administration. "It's a meeting that lasts for a couple of hours — a 'let your hair down' kind of meeting. That's how we know what the administration is up to."

Administrators would fully consult with appropriate committees and faculty groups after the outlines of a program were developed, and faculty saw that, compared to a previous administration, "there's a lot more talking — plain talking — between committees and senior administrators. We all know what's going on." Administrators not only talked but also listened, so that faculty believed that their counsel, while only advisory, was highly influential. One faculty leader noted that "the administration has been able to pick up and take the lead on [faculty concerns], and that's the way it should be."

Managing Renewal

The planning process at Research College was developed and implemented in a top-down fashion. It was designed by the president and senior staff, and then presented to faculty representative bodies for their review. While there was a great deal of interaction within the university, it tended to occur within discrete role-related groups rather than through groups that cut across many roles. For example, the senior administrative staff viewed itself as a team that met at least once a week; as one administrator said, "The top management team here is very important." Team members, in turn, would meet with members of their own staffs.

The president's planning and program review process was characterized by one faculty member as based more on a corporate than a collegial ideology. At the same time, the faculty member acknowledged that faculty governance had remained intact and that administrative leadership, from the president on down, was very concerned with working with faculty. He said, "It will be O.K. as long as the administration responds to faculty comments."

The program review process was integrated into the institution's management systems and was predicated on self-assessments by individual departments, which led to the development of implementation plans and yearly follow-ups. The reviews also included analyses by both internal and external teams. The reviews were guided centrally by a set of highly structured written protocols and were coordinated by a campuswide faculty-administration committee, whose members also participated in the individual reviews. The review results were understood by all to influence decision making and resource allocations. At the same time, the reviews were considered confidential between the administration and each department, so that no department was publicly embarrassed or identified as deficient. Unlike at State College, however, the reviews were closely monitored at the institutional level. Reviews, warts and all, moved up through the administrative hierarchy and were eventually discussed by the trustees.

Empirical data were considered very important at Research College, and the institution in general had increasingly engaged in systematic analyses of policies and procedures previously taken for granted. Extensive reports, in which longitudinal and comparative data featured prominently, were prepared on emerging issues. Some of these reports were considered confidential and not widely distributed, but those privy to them continually referred to their findings. These reports, initiated by the administration, tied together historical and contemporary data on matters the president thought important and provided the core for a campus agenda.

Institutional Values

The culture of Research College emphasized meritocratic quality and civility. The planning and program review processes were consistent with campus and professional values, although these values were quite different from those at State College. Research College faculty accepted strong administrative leadership as long as they felt that the faculty voice was heard and respected and essential academic values were being protected.

At Research College, the planning process determined that some departments and programs were of greater long-term significance to the academic development of the campus than others and therefore should receive additional resources. The program assessment process was related both to strategic planning and to budget allocations, so that there was a potential for departments to be winners or losers. As long as these processes were visible to faculty, and emphasized meritocratic criteria, they were accepted as consistent with the institution's concern for merit and quality.

Although the president was highly directive in designing the program, presidential initiative was accepted because it accurately reflected the desires of the constituents. One trustee said that the president's contribution to the renewal was a "master plan to get us from where we were to where he thought the university could go. [There] was a vision shared by trustees and faculty, but there was no plan to get there." The president therefore didn't create the vision, but rather created a direct linkage in people's minds between the comparatively inchoate goals in which they believed and the highly structured program he developed.

Propositions for Renewing Institutions

What are the important ingredients for renewing institutions? Generalizations based on an analysis of programs at just two hand-picked institutions are of course highly tentative. Nevertheless, the case data suggest the possibility that some institutional elements play only an insignificant role while others are crucial.

Certain factors which appeared in one program but not the other may not be absolutely essential. Programs leading to campuswide renewal may be successful in institutions that are public or private, unionized or nonunionized. They may em-

phasize student learning or scholarly productivity as in the two
colleges described here; other themes, such as service to a local
community or specific clientele, can serve as well (Birnbaum,
1989d). They may be developed from the top down or from the
bottom up; they may function effectively in a centralized or decentralized manner; they may stress empirical data or ignore
them; and they may be integrated into other management systems or isolated from them. They may require additional fiscal
resources, or be accomplished within the constraints of existing budgets. They may be developed in institutions with presidents who are either new or long term, cosmopolitan or local,
and whose boards see themselves as institutional supporters or
as campus watchdogs. Neither the presence nor absence of any
of these conditions would appear necessary to institutional renewal. However, other factors, present in both institutions, may
be related to the success of renewal programs.

Presidential Leadership

Successful and systemic institutional renewal programs require
legitimated presidents who can exercise power without inducing alienation. Both presidents were self-assured, articulate, and
considered vigorous administrative and educational leaders by
their colleagues. They were acknowledged to have expertise of
a high order and were at once admired and respected by their
faculty colleagues and administration subordinates. In terms of
factors considered in earlier chapters, both presidents had previously been faculty members, had directive theories of leadership, emphasized active search, avoided both linear and adaptive
strategy, emphasized interpretive strategy, and were cognitively
complex.

Neither president appeared overly conscious of status.
While they recognized the importance of their positions and appeared comfortable in exercising power, both occupied unim-
posing offices, seemed relatively indifferent to the perquisites
of position, and could jokingly deprecate their influence and discuss their achievements with some modesty. Both had extensive presidential experience, the president of State College with

long tenure in one setting and the president of Research College with shorter tenure but in several settings. In addition to having the influence that accompanied the authority of their office, both were seen as expert and as likable and could therefore influence others without inducing alienation. The presidents also listened to others, allowed themselves to be influenced, and were seen as seeking the opinions of others and making principled decisions.

On any campus there are many issues that call for administrative attention. As they respond to the changing demands for their time, leaders often remove themselves from concern or active involvement with ongoing programs. The programs at both campuses were successful because the presidents continued to give extensive personal attention to them.

There were several circumstances that promoted that attention. It is not surprising that the president of State College, who had relatively few opportunities to play a national educational statesman role, was on campus all the time. But even the cosmopolitan president of Research College, who had continual opportunities to leave the campus for extended periods, did not do so. Both presidents were more concerned with internal than with external affairs, and both focused their attention on the campus and the strength of its academic programs. In addition, both presidents were persistent in promoting their programs and committed to monitoring their progress. The president of State College said, "I'm very persistent in pushing my ideas; I don't forget them even if I don't get what I want right away. I know that eventually I'll outlast [my opponents]. I'll be here longer than they will. It might take years, but eventually I'll get these things." The president of Research College commented, "Leadership is hard work. You cannot articulate a global vision and walk away. The real problem of leadership is translating it into practical things. You don't have to be a genius — it just requires paying attention."

Both presidents emphasized building on strength, rather than correcting weakness. They believed that their faculty were hardworking and of high quality, and that campus programs were strong. While both presidents were aware that some individuals were not as involved as they might be, this was seen

"My problem was I kept reading books on leadership and excellence and management when I should have been working."

Source: Drawing by James Stevenson. Reprinted by permission of James Stevenson from *Harvard Business Review,* 1987.

as the exception rather than the rule, and they both recognized that the faculty were the heart of the enterprise. They saw the purpose of their programs as improving academic activities that were already sound, rather than correcting deficiencies. Constituent groups could participate in these programs enthusiastically, because doing so was a source of pride and satisfaction rather than an acknowledgment of weakness.

Sharing Leadership

Successful programs of institutional renewal depend on shared governance and reciprocal influence. The processes of both institutions were characterized by adherence to concepts of shared authority. At both institutions, expectations of mutual influence permitted both faculty and administration to feel that their interests were protected. This made it possible for them to work together collaboratively and nondefensively. The processes through which this was achieved were quite different, emphasizing joint action on one campus and accountability on the other, but the outcome was similar; in both institutions, faculty shared ownership of the programs.

Shared authority at State College was exhibited through joint action that limited administrative discretion but led to mutually satisfactory results. Union and senate leaders were involved in all major decisions, and the president viewed this relationship as essential to the implementation of his ideas and the smooth operation of the campus. In the assessment program, for example, the president said, "I got strong and thoughtful people from the union and put them in leadership positions. It would have been impossible for the program to succeed without union support. You can't separate bargaining and academic affairs." Lines between faculty and administration were often blurred by releasing faculty from their teaching positions to assume administrative responsibility for assessment program activities. The consequence of shared authority at State College was that people felt empowered.

At Research College, shared authority was provided by communication and accountability. Administrators listened to faculty, developed programs they believed faculty would support, and consulted with faculty and were responsive to their counsel. Administrative discretion was maximized because administrators were sensitive to faculty concerns. One administrator said, "People are satisfied with the governance structure. It provides for consultation, but the president makes decisions and tells people why." The consequences of shared authority at Research College were that people felt informed and able to hold administrators accountable. A faculty member commented that "the administration listens to the faculty. They don't always agree, but you get a hearing, and you are listened to and respected."

As a consequence of respectful listening at both institutions, faculty and administrators were able to assert and strengthen their ownership of the programs even as they told conflicting stories about how the programs were started. At State College, the program was believed by many to have been initiated by the president. As one board leader said, "There is no question about it. These were the president's ideas." At the same time, faculty leaders told a somewhat different story in which the union was responsible both for developing the program and for getting a reluctant president to accept it. At Research College, an administrative leader said that the program "was really developed by the president, a top-down plan," while a faculty leader said that "the program review committee was our idea—we needed accountability. It was not the president's idea."

Institutional Values

Successful programs of institutional renewal must be consistent with existing institutional values in their idealized form. Both institutions had strong cultures with key values exemplified by the values of their presidents. Both presidents understood the history and respected the cultures of their colleges. They were seen as totally committed to the kind of education represented by their institutions and considered by their constituents as exemplars of core institutional values. The president at State College, for example, identified institutions such as his as "the anvils of democracy." He suggested that institutions such as Research College were relatively unimportant; it was because of institutions such as State College that the United States as a nation would or would not "make it." The president of Research College, in turn, described how he had been prepared for his position through his past experiences in an institution whose rigorous academic environment had given him "a refined and clean sense of academic excellence."

The program developed at State College reflected the institution's concern for the undergraduate curriculum and student development and diversity. It enabled faculty and administrators to continue to work together in collaborative fashion, separated the program from other institutional control mechanisms, and protected the faculty from invidious comparisons. The program at Research College emphasized quality, assessment against universal meritocratic standards, and peer review. It permitted the administration to direct the process and integrate it into institutional control systems. In terms of focus, process, or structure, neither program would have been successful if an attempt had been made to implement it at the other institution.

Each program involved reviews of academic programs by the faculty responsible for developing and teaching them, as well as peer review of that process, and both these activities were consistent with general academic values. The major purpose of each program was to strengthen the college's academic core, a goal that faculty and administrators alike could support. Fiscal benefits that might accrue were considered as secondary outcomes and not as primary motivations.

At State College, the view was that "we don't look at assessment as an accountability mechanism, but as a learning tool. We're helping faculty to improve." At Research College, resource allocation decisions were structured as responses to issues of quality rather than as attempts to induce savings.

The definition of success and the motivation of departments toward self-improvement differed at the two colleges. At State College, success was the extent to which students met the specific learning objectives that each department had uniquely defined. At Research College, success was judged through data analyses and extensive internal and external review procedures that indicated good management, high quality, and student satisfaction. At both institutions, administrators were strong public advocates of the institution's progress, faculty had great pride in the college's accomplishments, and presidential pronouncements constantly kept the program visible and salient to the campus community.

Renewal and Autonomy

The programs at both institutions were initiated by internal leaders in response to their perceptions of institutional needs. Neither institution was under an external mandate to develop its program. The design of each program was idiosyncratic, accommodated a number of diverse views, and served multiple purposes.

The organic, self-directed nature of the programs was mentioned by leaders on both campuses as a major factor in their success. At State College, for example, one leader said, "The purpose of assessment is to get faculty to *think* about what they are doing and why—that's less likely to happen if it is externally imposed. It's not a mechanical process." The difference between a program imposed by others and one self-imposed was seen in the outcomes. The former challenges people to follow the rules; the latter challenges them "to be more resourceful and independent in what they are doing—to maximize their commitment to the enterprise."

Successful programs of institutional renewal must be internally developed and designed. They cannot be externally imposed. Most of what is produced in higher education is a result of faculty activity. When attempts to strengthen institutions are seen by the faculty as inconsistent with their interests, they often lead to reduced morale and effort rather than improvement. Externally imposed strategies may reduce the faculty's sense of participation, demean their professional status, and make them merely employees.

The Limits to Leadership

Successful programs of institutional renewal may depend on conditions that cannot always be planned or replicated. Although the two presidents were highly skilled, program success at both institutions was related in some measure to chance events and fortuitous circumstances over which leaders had little control. The presence of these unpredictable factors may cause programs successful in one setting to fail in another for reasons that may have little to do with the quality of leadership.

At State College, for example, the president had supported the idea of student assessment for many years without having any effect on institutional programs. The unexpected availability of a source of external funding, in a format that was consistent with the assessment idea, provided an opportunity for program development that would not otherwise have been possible.

The president of Research College had the good fortune to

take office at a time of increasing fiscal difficulty. Many faculty thought the institution was drifting without a clear set of priorities, an accountable management system, or the ability to ensure uniformly high quality in its diverse programs. As one administrator reported, "There was a vague feeling that the faculty wanted direction," and a faculty committee finally submitted a report calling for increased accountability and a process for program review. When the new president took office, he was greeted with the unforeseen prospect of a faculty mandate for planning and program review. The development of this program was therefore interpreted by some, not as an administrative initiative, but as a dutiful administrative response to the expressed will of the faculty.

Institutional Renewal as Interpretation

Good presidential leadership may be a necessary, but not a sufficient, cause of institutional renewal. Presidential leadership is influenced by interacting webs of administrative routines, environmental pressures, and political processes that take place in the context of institutional history and culture.

Institutions constantly change, and these changes often lead to improvement. Sometimes these changes occur in subunits that are small and isolated and have little impact on the campus as a whole. Sometimes the changes are inconsistent with campus culture and wither owing to faculty indifference or administrative neglect. When campus cultures are weak, or when leaders have lost the ability to influence the symbolic life of the campus, even presidents who know and care about these improvements may be unable to get others to see them as worthy of support.

But when presidents maintain the ability to influence others, they may be able to create linkages between a new program that they support and the core values already present in a strong institutional culture. Other subunits come to see the program's purposes as consistent with their own interests, success in one part of the program creates infectious enthusiasm that cascades through the institution, and the college is ripe for renewal. Programs with the potential to renew colleges require good management and must eventually be supported by significant structural and administrative change if they are to be effective. But good management is more a consequence than a cause of institutional improvement. And improvement cannot occur as a result of a legislative mandate, a board edict, or a presidential order. Renewal is possible when people at a college develop a sense of institutional loyalty, feelings of shared responsibility and respect, and a commitment to common academic values. Renewal comes from the ability of presidents to interpret reality for their constituencies. Developing programs that give concrete expression to core institutional values moves constituents toward more common goals. Testimony at both State College and Research College was unanimous in asserting that their programs had significantly increased — and focused — the activity level of both faculty and administration. Administrators and faculty leaders spent time on these programs because they came to be seen as representing the essential character of their campuses. The success of the programs became a symbol of the success of the institutions.

PART THREE

Improving
Academic Leadership

CHAPTER 8

When Presidents Are Important

A major purpose of leadership is to help organizational participants develop convergence and greater consistency in their actions and their views of reality and, in doing so, to bring a truce
to what Gardner (1990, p. 95) has called "the war of the parts
against the whole." Good leadership permits college constituents to maintain or move toward agreement on basic institutional norms and values, which in turn affects their willingness
to accept influence from others and increases their commitment
to the collective enterprise. People in a college, as in other organizations, wonder, What should we be doing? and, Why are
we all here together? Leadership helps to affirm an answer.

    College presidents can be important. When they are per-
ceived by their constituents as competent, legitimate, value-
driven, of complex mind, and open to influence, presidents can
be a vital source of leadership and a force for institutional renewal. At the same time, presidents are not the only source of
campus leadership, and colleges can improve even when presidents fail. In an academic institution, leadership can be provided
by others, and attention can be focused by history, culture, and
training. Even without presidents, leadership happens.

    ILP data can be used to support both the strong leader
and weak leader views of the academic presidency. How can
these two apparently conflicting views be reconciled? This chap-

ter will discuss the ways in which two factors — presidents and organizational processes that are only partially subject to presidential influence — interact and affect institutional coherence, improvement, and renewal.

Presidential Leadership

Organizations can be analyzed at two distinct levels, substantive and symbolic. The substantive dimension involves understanding how decisions and other organizational actions result in observable, objective outcomes. The symbolic aspect focuses on how organizational activities are perceived, interpreted, and legitimated (Pfeffer, 1981). Presidents can influence their institutions on both levels — through instrumental leadership, which makes some things more visible and obvious, and through interpretive leadership, which makes some things more desirable. Although these two forms of leadership are conceptually distinct, they interact with each other; instrumental acts often have symbolic significance, and interpretive acts affect the way people behave and think. All acts of presidential leadership involve both forms of leadership, but to varying degrees.

Instrumental Leadership

College presidents provide instrumental leadership through their technical competence, experience, and judgment. They coordinate the activities of others, make timely and sensible decisions, represent the institution to its various publics, and cope with the everyday crises caused by environmental change and internal conflict. These are complex responsibilities, but most presidents move through careers that prepare them to accomplish these tasks at an acceptable level of performance. By the time they become viable candidates for presidencies, they have developed an understanding of the intricacies of institutional processes such as budgeting, planning, and community relations sufficient to permit them to monitor institutional performance and initiate corrections or changes. They have had ex-

perience in the exercise of authority, feel confident in their judgments, and have been socialized into the field of higher education in general (and most likely also into the general values of
institutions similar to the one which they now head).

Presidents are generally highly intelligent and proficient in
the technical skills demanded by the job. If, on average, presidents
don't seem to make much of a difference to institutional outcomes,
it may not be because they are weak. In fact, their ability to provide
instrumental leadership is in general at a high level. Just as most
physicians are likely to have similar degrees of success in treat-
ing most common ailments, most presidents properly fulfill the
instrumental requirements of their roles. They are able to engage in behaviors that keep the institution going, assure its responsiveness to a changing environment, improve its programs at the
margin, and make effective use of institutional resources.

Instrumental leadership is an indispensable ingredient of
institutional effectiveness, with both practical and symbolic consequences. In strong institutions with high morale, good instrumental leadership may bolster confidence, permeate the college with new initiatives and creative ideas, and lead to general
satisfaction and pride. In troubled institutions at which people
feel depressed and beleaguered, good instrumental leadership
may correct obvious inefficiencies, repair ruptured external support systems, and keep hope alive by demonstrating that even
in times of difficulty it is possible to improve. Because of the
decentralized nature of academic authority, presidents usually
share instrumental leadership with a large number of other constituents, making it possible even for those institutions with less
competent presidents to operate effectively. Nevertheless, presidents have a particularly important influence on instrumental
leadership because they control resources, play a central role
in communication networks, and serve as institutional representative to the world outside the campus. Because college constituents recognize the legitimacy of administrative authority and
are able to judge the technical quality of decisions, presidents
may be able to provide effective instrumental leadership even
in the absence of strong constituent support.

Interpretive Leadership

If instrumental leadership does the best it can with the institution as it is, interpretive leadership involves altering perceptions of institutional functioning and the relationship of the institution to its environment. This kind of leadership emphasizes the "management of meaning" through actions or words of the leader that "guide the attention of those involved in a situation in ways that are consciously or unconsciously designed to shape the meaning of the situation" (Smircich and Morgan, 1982, p. 261). Interpretation is a moral act of leadership that should not be confused with the immoral act of distortion. Interpretation involves clarifying and explaining the connections between leader behavior, institutional beliefs, and transcendental values. Distortion means deliberately misrepresenting and casting false light on leader behavior to make it appear acceptable even though it does not truly further a college's higher purposes. Interpretation builds commitment to communal values; distortion produces cynicism and self-interest.

Interpretive leadership that affects individual subunits of a college can come from many sources. But interpretive leadership that influences an entire institution can usually come only from presidents, although the special characteristics of colleges sometimes make it possible for academic vice presidents to provide interpretive leadership as well. Presidents, by virtue of their hierarchical positions and legitimacy, are believed by others to have a coherent sense of the institution and are therefore permitted if not expected to articulate institutional purposes. Presidents can instill or renew pride in the institution as they attend to symbolic acts, serve as a focal point for a new beginning, or are identified, as was one ILP president, as "Mr. College" and serve as the institution's living embodiment of purpose.

Presidents provide interpretive leadership when they change perceptions by highlighting some aspects of the institution and environment while muting others, by relating new ideas to existing values and symbols, and by articulating a vision of the college in idealized form that captures what others believe but have been unable to express. Changing perceptions in this

*"Well, actually, I <u>don't</u> know whither bound.
But it's better than letting the impression get around that we're adrift."*

Source: Drawing by Ed Fisher. Reprinted by permission of Ed Fisher from *Harvard Business Review,* 1991.

way is difficult in a professional environment. On the one hand, there is a natural tendency for people in all organizations to look toward those in leadership roles for guidance in making sense of a confusing and chaotic world. People want their organizations to be "understandable, predictable, and manageable" (Bolman and Deal, 1984, p. 13). On the other hand, professionals are trained to rely on their own perceptions and to resist attempts by authority to influence their judgment. Faculty are likely to permit their perceptions of reality to be swayed only when they believe the president understands and represents their interests, listens to them, and is responsive to their influence.

Although it is possible to identify factors that may make it more or less likely that a president may be able to provide interpretive leadership, there is no formula that will guarantee it. Unlike instrumental leadership, interpretive leadership cannot be exercised without constituent support. But even those well thought of may not be able to influence others' perceptions of reality. A president's ability to do that depends not only on being seen as sharing values and understanding the culture, but also on ineffable personality characteristics, timing, and luck, culminating in a fortuitous match between the individual's characteristics and institutional characteristics.

When all of these factors are present, presidents can help institutions see their values and activities in different ways. At many colleges, for example, academic departments resent program review activities; they see them as time-wasting and contrary to their basic values of autonomy and academic freedom. At State College and Research College (described in Chapter Seven), however, regular program assessments were embraced as visible manifestations of the deeply felt values of student development and meritocratic quality to which the program's presidential proponents had linked them. Because almost any program initiative has the potential to be associated with one or another academic or institutional value, a president with a deep understanding of institutional history and culture may profoundly affect what an institution does and the reasons constituents give for its actions.

Although it might appear that opportunities to influence perceptions of reality occur only when dealing with abstract matters, in fact, often the most mundane and concrete aspects of institutional life have great potential for interpretation. Budgets, for example, are the lifeblood of a college. They are the academic program in money terms; they represent the outcomes of political battles won and lost; and yet they are completely ambiguous documents. Most faculty cannot understand budgets because they do not have the skills or time to do so — the documents are too complex, and they cannot cognitively manage the crosswalk between the numbers and the reality they see. They therefore have to rely on others' interpretations of what the budget "means" (Neumann, in press). Presidents who merely report numbers to the faculty and believe that the budget speaks for itself forfeit an unusually potent opportunity to affect constituent perceptions of reality. A bad budget, for example, can be presented as a rallying cry for working more closely together and used as an opportunity to recount stories of past accomplishments under similarly desperate circumstances. Alternatively, it can be a cause for faultfinding and recrimination. Presidents can paint a budget as a temporary and relatively inconsequential pause when seen in the context of a history of institutional progress, or as a portent of an even more dreary future.

Instrumental and Interpretive Leadership and Presidential Paths

Linking the three paths followed by the ILP presidents to instrumental and interpretive leadership (as shown in Figure 2) provides further insight into these two forms of leadership.

Figure 2. Leadership and Presidential Paths.

Does the President Provide Instrumental Leadership?	Does the President Provide Interpretive Leadership?	
	Yes	No
Yes	Exemplary	Modal
No	----	Failed

Almost all presidents enter office with the potential to exercise interpretive leadership, but most cannot maintain it. Presidents begin their terms of office with strong support because of the development of "idiosyncrasy credits" (Hollander, 1985). They earn this credit, which is a form of political capital, because their previous experiences lead to attributions of expertise and because their selection by search committees with faculty representation provides their appointment with legitimation. Presidents continue to gain credit in the eyes of others if their constituents see them both as competent and as conforming to institutional norms and values. Presidents with credit have sufficient status to successfully innovate, take initiative, and influence organizational change that would not be accepted from a president without such credit. Constituents have the expectation that the new president will listen, be subject to influence, and be "one of us." Because organizational participants want to believe that the president will be a good leader, they ignore discordant evidence during the honeymoon period.

But as we saw in Chapter Five, this automatic process of positive attribution changes over time. It can be altered suddenly by a major incident involving precipitant behavior that causes immediate disaffection among large numbers of organizational participants, or it can be changed gradually as evidence of autocratic behavior accumulates and individuals with different thresholds of concern slowly evolve a new consensus of presidential ineffectiveness (Feldman, 1981). When followers' expectations of leaders are unfulfilled, leaders lose their credits, because "the leader who 'sits' on his or her credits may be seen as lacking the 'will' to take action in line with role obligations" (Hollander, 1985, p. 502). If faculty don't believe a president is doing well, it violates the transactional idea of leadership as a "fair exchange" in which leaders receive esteem and responsiveness from constituents in exchange for providing them with a sense of direction, recognition, and values (Hollander, 1987, p. 14).

Exemplary presidents have retained their ability to influence both the way their institutions are managed and the interpretations that define the reality of other organizational participants. They do not attempt to change institutional values as much as they stress and renew certain values already present in the institution. Exemplary presidents give equal attention to tasks and relationships, and have a collaborative relationship with the faculty. Their continued willingness to listen and be influenced serves as a source of renewal of their moral authority and interpretive capabilities.

Modal presidents can manage institutional processes but have lost the ability to affect the interpretive life of the campus. Modal presidents start off concerned with both tasks and people, but over time lose sight of people and emphasize tasks. They become disengaged from the faculty, but retain the support of other constituencies. They listen less and pronounce more, and their openness to influence diminishes. Their sense of reality becomes increasingly different from that of the faculty, and they forgo the opportunity to renew the interpretive influence with which they entered.

Failed presidents lose the ability to constructively influence either institutional processes or symbolic interpretations. Failed presidents develop an adversarial relationship with the faculty that may later affect the support of other constituencies as well.

Although the model in Figure 2 suggests the possibility of presidents who exercise interpretive but not instrumental leadership, there were no examples in the ILP sample. Because the careers of presidential aspirants usually include promotions based on instrumental achievements at lower organizational levels, this category of leader, although not unknown, is atypical in higher education.

Organizational Factors Affecting the Importance of the President

Individuals can provide leadership as they focus the attention of others through their instrumental or interpretive acts. But ILP data suggest that four other organizational elements focus people's attention and influence the way they interpret reality as well. The culture and history of an institution facilitate some actions and circumscribe others. Succession cycles can act as a surrogate for presidential leadership. Structure can restrict presidential leadership. And several types of self-perpetuating processes establish the limits within which presidents can successfully act.

Culture and History

Institutional culture and history play a major role in determining what a president can do. Schein (1985, p. 313) has argued that "once an organization has evolved a mature culture because it has a long and rich history, that culture creates the patterns of perception, thought, and feeling of every new generation in the organization, and, therefore, also 'causes' the organization to be predisposed to certain kinds of leadership. In that sense, the mature group, through its culture, also creates its own leaders."

What institutions have done in the past may therefore have a profound influence over what their leaders can do today. For example, at many ILP campuses, changes in institutional purpose or mission made years earlier during the heady days of higher education growth created conflicts that continued to influence campus life. One president ruefully noted that "our strength, but also our liability, is that we recruited a bright young faculty fifteen years ago, and they got caught in the academic crunch. They had not planned to stay, but they are still here. The faculty is split. There is an activist core made up of faculty from arts and sciences. They want the college to be different from what it is, that it have more graduate education and more research and all the trappings that go with research."

This kind of conflict — manifesting itself on different campuses as traditionalists versus activists, teacher education versus liberal arts, advocates of campus "family" versus supporters of "standards," or haves versus have-nots — was a conspicuous element of campus governance at many institutions in the ILP, particularly in the public sector. At some institutions, many such groups flourished, each with its own leaders. At other institutions, such conflicts inhibited the emergence of leadership.

The multiplicity of leaders in a college could either significantly enhance or severely restrict presidential influence. What presidents can do as leaders may depend on what they are permitted to do by other leaders. The greatest challenge of presidential leadership is not to control the organization but to bring the interpretations of these other leaders into closer alignment with the interpretations of the president. When such alignments are developed, as they were at State College and Research College, presidential, board, administrative, and faculty leadership reinforce one another, and presidential influence is strengthened. When this does not happen, as on campuses with failed presidents, constituents try to obtain their own objectives through power and manipulation, further weakening presidential influence.

History can also focus attention and provide present-day actions with meaning. A previous transition from emphasizing teaching to emphasizing research at one ILP institution had led to problems in instruction, governance, and morale. Released time for research led to increasing class size, and professors hired prior to the change complained that teaching didn't matter any more. But the institution's history intervened, and a faculty leader described how, "recently, there's been a recognition that we can't forget our primary goal of undergraduate education. The reason I ran for senate is my concern for the upset of the research-teaching balance. My platform was to bring undergraduate education back into perspective and give it the same emphasis as research." This institutional memory led to the development of a new college emphasis on general education.

Presidential Succession Cycles

The presidential succession cycle described in Chapters Four and Five provides evidence that certain organizational *processes* can, in the short term, provide the same increases in college morale, enthusiasm, and perceptions of improvement that are usually considered a consequence of leadership.

As we have seen, most presidents do not have strong faculty support at the time they leave office. The selection of the successor president is seen by constituents as representing a new beginning, and the selection process and its successful conclusion are likely to generate a high level of institutional enthusiasm. The arrival of the new president itself symbolizes institutional change and improvement. Presidents enter office with new ideas, alter the administrative hierarchy, and develop new administrative procedures. Old processes can no longer be taken for granted, dormant ideas are reawakened, and perceptions of what is real and what is possible are altered.

ILP data indicated not only that presidents at the beginning of their terms enjoy higher constituent support than those who had been in office for longer periods, but that new presidents are also likely to be associated with campus improvement as seen both by faculty and by researchers. This appeared to be true independent of the path that the president will ultimately take. In other words, campuses are seen to improve as a consequence of succession, regardless of the characteristics of the successor. For example, when presidents were unchanged between the first and second campus visits, researchers were more likely to rate the campuses of new presidents as improved (eight of fourteen) than the campuses of old presidents (one of seven). Researchers also rated the campuses of transitional presidents (who had left or were about to leave) as more improved (eight of eleven) than the campuses of continuing presidents (nine of twenty-one), indicating the important effects of presidential replacements. Therefore, changes that appear to be induced by a new president may instead be a consequence of a predictable, cyclical college process of renewal symbolized by administrative succession. Unwary new presidents might incorrectly take signs of an improved campus as a confirmation of the effectiveness of their behavior, rather than as a common and expected campus response to presidential succession. Campus improvements observed when presidents leave are further evidence that, in general, leadership problems may be caused not by presidential terms that are too short, but terms that are too long.

Because the succession process not only leads to specific institutional changes but also to feelings of a new beginning, it serves both instrumental and interpretive functions. The process may be a particularly important means for providing hope and authenticating core values in organizations like colleges that have few other ways of measuring their success, assessing their performance, or confirming their purposes.

Structural Considerations

ILP data suggest that two structural elements — the presence of a faculty union and membership in an institutional system — may reduce faculty support for a president and therefore constrain the leadership that the president can exercise. Neither element makes good leadership impossible, however, and in fact, exemplary presidents were found both on unionized and system-related campuses.

ILP interviews did not provide a great deal of data to indicate why, on average, presidents on unionized campuses enjoyed less faculty support than other presidents. It may be related to the tendency of traditional bargaining structures to inhibit, rather than enhance, informal communications, thereby weakening a president's ability to provide interpretive leadership.

The problems associated with institutional system membership were articulated with much greater clarity. Presidents were more likely to be supported by constituents when they were seen as subject to influence from below. But influence from below can be effective only to the extent that the person influenced is in turn able to influence those above (Smith and Peterson, 1988). When the president has little control over decisions because they are made above the campus level, attempts to influence the president are seen by faculty as meaningless.

Exasperated ILP interviewees described numerous instances of system decisions that inhibited presidential leadership. For example, public institutions were often mandated to carry out particular missions by the state, leading to funding for some programs and not others. Regardless of the economic justification for such decisions, they had the effect of reducing morale by creating have and have-not faculty and limiting the opportunities for institutional initiative. Institutional systems could also make rules and regulations that were outside presidential control and caused great anxiety and anger. For example, one system required a campus on the quarter system to replan its curriculum to operate on a semester system. After completing the exercise, the system reversed its decision. Other campuses found themselves faced with system-mandated changes in admissions or graduation requirements, in programs, or in budget allocations. The issue for system intervention is not whether the system decisions in these instances were "right," but the degree to which, through circumscribing campus decision making, they also limited the emergence of campus leadership and exacerbated president-faculty tensions.

Because institutional systems could impose numerous and conflicting constraints on presidents, there was always something about these presidents that could be criticized. One ILP president, who took over an institution that ranked near the bottom on all attributes considered important by the system, decided to focus his immediate attention on interacting with leaders off campus rather than those on campus. As a consequence, he achieved extraordinary results in terms of student recruitment, external funding, and public visibility, all of which strengthened both institutional performance and institutional morale. But the cost of attending to external audiences was less attention given to problematic administrative issues that the system also considered important, so the president was still criticized for lax management controls, problematic audits, and reports not submitted on time.

Presidents working in systems were likely to bridle at the restrictions. In describing campus-system relationships, one president said, "There are bad and good things. I can't think of anything that is good about them now."

Self-Reinforcing Processes

The interlocking loops of campus interaction and influence that develop over time lead to self-reinforcing or self-correcting processes that make colleges stable and difficult for leaders to change (Birnbaum, 1988a). They create routines of beliefs, culture, and knowledge, as well as routines of procedures, rules, and strategies, that "are independent of the actors who execute them and capable of surviving considerable turnover in individual actors" (Levitt and March, 1988, p. 320). These routines created by culture and procedures also continually reinforce the culture and the procedures, embedding them more firmly in the institution. Routines are reflections of a college's values, traditions, history, and governance systems. They also influence the paths taken by college presidents. Although these processes may be invisible when the campus is running as people expect, they become activated and evident when various constituents come to believe that things are not going the way they should. An institution's self-correcting processes can focus attention, make certain outcomes more likely than others, and either support or thwart the intentions of a president.

An especially coherent culture contains processes that can strengthen an institution, but that can also act as a brake to presidential intentions. One ILP institution, whose trustees were predominantly graduates of the college and whose administrators came from the faculty ranks, found it difficult to respond to budget problems involving staffing commitments to departments. The coherent culture meant that discussions about whether a specific vacant faculty position should be filled were apt to be tied in to other campus issues, such as the role of interdisciplinary studies, previous personnel decisions, the support of the vice president for academic affairs, or the role of faculty in governance. This compounded the difficulty of making changes desired by many campus leaders.

Governance structures could also develop into self-reinforcing systems beyond presidential control. Once expectations were shaped by history, they became difficult to change, and current problems were sometimes discussed and related to disputes decades earlier between faculty and long-since retired presidents or provosts. At one ILP institution, the president was trying, with limited success, to rebuild a faculty senate that had previously been a rubber stamp. A faculty leader noted that the senate "continues to operate under these constraints even though there has been an open invitation from the president to take part in the governance of the institution. It may be the goldfish bowl syndrome — when goldfish who have spent their lives in the goldfish bowl are put in a stream, they still swim in a circle."

Lee (1991) described the self-perpetuating factors that could lead senate-administration leadership either toward collaboration or disruption. At one ILP institution with comparatively effective governance, histories of strong faculty participation, administrative support, and positive relationships were all present and mutually reinforcing, so that the senate could become an instrument of institutional development and change. At another institution, administrators didn't defer to the senate or include its leaders in institutional management. This behavior both caused and was caused by a negative culture and overly complex structures that inhibited change. As Lee points out (pp. 47–48), "this intertwining of the three dimensions [of faculty participation, administrative support, and past relationships] made it difficult for either faculty leaders or administrators to improve governance relationships that had been historically poor."

Situations like this exemplify both the difficulties that even the best leaders may face when they try to influence their institutions and the limits to leadership. They suggest why the seductive cries for "stronger leadership" are so often empty; the functioning of an institution is based on the interaction of a number of critical factors, many of which are not under a president's control. Leadership is not a power to be wielded but a process of interaction to be nurtured.

Assessing the Importance of Presidential Leadership

Although an understanding of presidential leadership can be informed by research and analysis, assessing its importance is ultimately a matter of judgment. The effects that presidents may have on a campus are confounded by the actions of other institutional leaders, changes in the environment, and internal organizational processes such as culture and history that are difficult to change. Presidents are major participants in institutional events that have important organizational consequences, such as succession, but in many ways they follow common scripts and play roles that are independent of their own personal characteristics. Common cognitive biases may lead some observers to see the effects of leadership where it does not exist, or to ignore it when it does. And since leadership is what people think it is, assessments depend on the values of the observer. Given all of these problems, what can be said about the importance of presidential leadership?

In general, presidents appear capable of providing appropriate instrumental leadership to their campuses. Most of the time, most presidents attend to tasks and relationships in a manner that supports institutional objectives. Their leadership behavior in this regard is not tightly connected to institutional performance, and to this extent, who the president is makes little difference. This does not demean presidents, nor does it propose that *anyone* can be a president. Rather, it suggests that from the perspective of instrumental leadership, institutional fortunes are not likely to be altered significantly if a campus has as president one carefully selected and experienced person rather than another.

However, the same cannot be said of the capacity of presidents to provide interpretive leadership. The clearest examples of the effects of interpretive leadership were seen in the development of the campuses of the four exemplary old presidents. Each institution underwent significant programmatic or structural change during the president's tenure, each campus was conspicuously successful when compared with similar institutions, and faculty attributed campus success to the president's leadership. These data are still equivocal about the importance of presidents. They do not indicate, for example, whether exemplary presidents created campus improvement, or campus improvement created exemplary presidents. Nevertheless, they offer the possibility that while presidential leadership may have only a marginal effect on institutions most of the time, it potentially may have a major effect in renewing institutional values and improving organizational performance under certain conditions.

While the campuses of exemplary presidents can be used to argue the importance of strong presidential leadership, the campuses of modal presidents tell a somewhat different story. Although faculty support of the modal president was lower, most modal presidents were still able to manage their institutions effectively. Modal presidents, although not loved by the faculty, could still be respected, and as long as the support of trustees and administrative colleagues was maintained, they could influence through the use of legitimate power, reward power, and expert power (French and Raven, 1968). Often, even severe critics commented that the institution had improved under the leadership of presidents not liked by faculty.

On one campus on which the president did not have strong faculty support, a faculty leader who described the president as authoritarian and autocratic went on to say that he was effective and that "the campus is better off than it would have been with the leadership of another president." At another campus with a modal president, similar opposing views were simultaneously expressed. On the one hand, people said, "She straightened out the financial problems. She got the campus a new building. She was very supportive of the college. She did well in the state capitol. She did a lot for the image of the college. She was an excellent public speaker. People felt her perspective was full of enthusiasm. She made things happen." At the same time, others noted, "She had alienated a number of faculty. There was no confidence in her academic backing; she had no real, traditional academic experience. She was too optimistic and she could not always deliver, mainly because of the political process. Many lost confidence in her."

The evidence on the effects of different presidential paths is conflicting. This is because the ability of leaders to influence organizational interpretations that lead to satisfaction may be only loosely coupled to their ability to influence substantive organizational outcomes (Pfeffer, 1981). At least over the short term, therefore, erosion of faculty support for a president need not significantly diminish the college's effectiveness.

However, if short-term support of the president may be of little consequence, faculty support of a president over the long run may strengthen positive attributions of leadership and enhance the president's ability to influence the interpretations of others. If leadership is socially constructed, then attributions of good leadership — and perhaps an enhanced willingness to accept the leader's perceptions of reality — may depend on how the leader is viwed by others. Bensimon (1990b) described how new presidents at two ILP institutions reduced status differences between themselves and the faculty, allowed themselves to be influenced, reflected back the faculty's ideas, and publicly advocated faculty interests in external forums. As a consequence, faculty came to see them as "one of us;" they attributed institutional successes to presidential leadership, were forgiving of presidential mistakes or weaknesses, and were accepting of presidential initiatives for campus change.

When Do Presidents Make a Difference?

The analysis in this chapter leads to several conclusions.

- Most presidents have short-term, marginal, positive, instrumental effects on their colleagues; these effects would likely not be different under another president with similar qualifications.
- In the short term, effective instrumental activities of presidents satisfy the basic leadership needs of most colleges.
- Over the long term, colleges also need the inspiration and motivation of interpretive leadership. This can be provided in two ways. Occasionally it is provided by an exemplary president who is seen as taking the role of faculty, listening, respecting the culture, and being subject to influence. The legitimation and support developed by these presidents may permit them powerful episodic leverage to renew their colleges. More frequently, interpretive leadership arises from the succession process itself, which creates hope, excitement, and perceptions of new beginnings, as the college in effect renews itself. This suggests that modal presidents may be "good enough," as long as they are not in office for extended periods.
- Failed presidents, who take a linear view of administration, act preemptively or in an authoritarian manner, and fail to listen or to be seen as being influenced by others, are likely to have small, negative, marginal effects on an institution over the short term. However, over the long term, the lack of faculty support leaves them unable to capitalize on institutional potential and makes their campuses dreary and often contentious places to work.

These conclusions suggest that those who argue that institutions — and perhaps higher education as a whole — will suffer irreparable damage if the presidential role is not uniformly enacted at the highest levels of performance are wrong. They give too much attention to the limited influence of a single individual, and too little to the activities of countless others engaged in leadership throughout the institution. They expect too many to exhibit the magic that only a few can possess. They overlook the great strengths to be found in institutional histories, traditions, and faculty preparation. They ignore the reality that the quality of teaching, or of research, depends primarily on the activities of individual faculty and is in most circumstances unrelated to presidential performance.

If they are to be effective, presidents must fulfill the functions of all good leaders (Hollander, 1987); they must be seen as conforming to institutional norms and contributing to the achievement of the institution's main tasks. The ability to renew institutional purpose or direct major institutional change through the use of interpretive strategy may be critical to institutions under certain circumstances, but may not ordinarily be important. For most presidents, most of the time, the linear and adaptive strategies available to them may be sufficient and appropriate for the exercise of leadership—"not the visionary, messianic program of a savior, but just the ordinary, everday kind of leadership of which most of us are capable: an acceptance of the burden of the responsibility along with a cheerful acceptance of our ignorance" (Johnson, 1989, p. 11).

CHAPTER 9

Lessons for Successful Leadership

Most colleges exist in changing environments that constantly challenge their operations and effectiveness. Some ILP colleges were subject to midyear budget rescissions, reductions in programs of state support, or spectacular losses in the value of their endowment. Some were required to alter expenditure patterns, raise tuition, or limit faculty salaries. Some were faced with the election of anti-education politicians, changes in public attitudes toward diversity, or legislation affecting governance.

Seemingly minor incidents could sometimes have consequences as great as those of a major political or economic event; a racial epithet scrawled on a campus building, or a ban by a local community on off-street parking, could lead to a painful reconsideration of campus values, changes in administrative structure, or divisive arguments over campus governance.

Leaders facing these unexpected and sometimes unprecedented changes could feel overwhelmed. As one senior administrator said, "Sometimes I feel like Winnie the Pooh being dragged by Christopher Robin with my head going bump, bump, bump down the stairs. There must be a better way, but my head hurts too much to think about it."

The major problem of presidential leadership in a turbulent environment is getting people to share a common sense of reality when, as a result of that environment, everyone's head

171

hurts too much to think about it. Because so much of presidential leadership depends on context, specific recommendations to increase presidential effectiveness made with no information about an institution's history, culture, or present circumstances are unlikely to be helpful.

Nevertheless, findings of the ILP suggest ten research-based principles of good academic leadership that can be offered to presidents with some confidence, even without knowing the specifics of their campuses. These principles involve making a good impression, knowing how to listen, balancing governance systems, avoiding simplistic thinking, de-emphasizing institutional bureaucracy, re-emphasizing core values, focusing on institutional strengths, encouraging others to be leaders, evaluating your own performance, and knowing when to leave. This chapter will examine the impact of each of these principles in some detail. That they may appear no more than common sense is a great strength, rather than a weakness. Experienced and successful presidents will, for the most part, recognize these principles as things they already know, even if the vicissitudes of administrative life make them difficult to implement. Nevertheless, presidents may be comforted by realizing that their wisdom is supported by research, and feel less pressured to succumb to the latest leadership fads.

Those whose actions are consistent with these principles are more likely than those who violate them to become exemplary presidents, and less likely to become failed presidents. Of course, nothing can guarantee success as a college president. But if the principles may not always help, at least they are unlikely to harm.

Make a Good First Impression

A college's first impressions of a new president are affected by both the selection process and the president's first actions. Errors in judgment made during these initial phases of a presidency can have lasting consequences.

The Selection Process

Presidents whose selection is not seen as legitimate by important constituencies — and particularly by the faculty — are at high risk for a failed presidency. Legitimacy is particularly critical for the faculty, because the exercise of leadership with this group does not depend on the power of the president but on the willingness of followers to accept influence (Hollander, 1985). Followers who do not accept the validity of the selection process are less likely to believe that presidential authority has been properly conferred.

Presidential candidates ordinarily may have little influence on the selection process itself, but if they suspect that important constituencies are likely to raise procedural questions later, they can protect themselves by either rejecting the offer of a presidency or asking to confer with those potentially disruptive constituencies prior to accepting. Since legitimation depends on the expectations of constituencies, no specific selection process can ensure it. In view of the wide acceptance of concepts of shared authority, however, candidates should be particularly wary of searches that do not involve representative faculty members.

Initial Actions

New college presidents go through an early learning process of defining their roles, determining the limits of their influence, and discovering what works. For presidents, taking charge involves not only the instrumental processes of making decisions, but also the interpretive processes of "making sense" of a new and equivocal environment. What presidents do cannot be separated from how they do it. Initial actions may have critical consequences for a president's tenure and first impressions may be difficult to change. Constituents will see what they have come to expect, so that early authoritarian actions may preclude later attempts by presidents to become more consultative.

Most new college presidents have not been previously associated with their institutions, nor have they been presidents before. The "job description" they have been given is usually so general in nature that it neither requires nor prohibits any potential presidential action. How should they approach their new role?

Based on her interviews with new presidents, Bensimon (1987, 1989b, 1990a) suggested that presidents might be better able to make sense of a new environment and function effectively within it if they visit the campus several times before beginning their terms. They should meet not just with trustees or major institutional officers but with many of the key faculty and administrative players as well. Presidents should carefully read critical documents such as policy manuals, personnel procedures, budgets, and state codes, not just to learn instrumental processes for getting things done, but also to avoid actions that violate established procedures or expected patterns of consultation.

It is easy for new presidents to immediately see institutional problems that need correction. New presidents are likely to believe that their institutions are not well run (Birnbaum, 1986) and to see previous organizational outcomes in a more negative way than did their predecessors (Levitt and March, 1988). They may be seduced into action by a belief that leadership requires them to *do* something to improve obvious weaknesses. Instead, presidents should take time to listen and learn before acting, and thereby avoid the common new-president syndrome of being "much too eager to find out what's wrong with the institution so they can have something to fix and feel that they are making an important contribution" (Bensimon, in press). This may help them avoid *inflicting* leadership on their campuses.

Taking time to make sense of college history and mood permits presidents to learn how people communicate, what they mean by the language they use, and what dreams and visions they have. Through interaction, presidents not only learn about others but help others to learn about presidential hopes and expectations. Making sense helps presidents understand others' expectations and gives them a better sense of the reactions their proposals are likely to generate. It helps presidents legitimize their leadership, and makes it more likely that they will be able to influence the reality of others.

In retrospect, ILP presidents justified their initial actions as necessary and appropriate and believed that others should do as they did. But they were unlikely to have an accurate perception of how others interpreted their first campus actions. One president, who engaged in immediate and dramatic action on taking office, recommended that other presidents should do the same, and said, "Most people wait a long time before they do anything, but a developing institution needs strong leadership. I have been accused of being autocratic and I admit it. I needed to say, 'This is what we had to do. When we get out of it, I can be more democratic.' I had to make sure we could clean up this place." He later found out, however, that his initial actions had inhibited campus movement toward shared authority. Another president, who acted quickly to effect change during her first years in office, noted how issues that seem critical on first taking office assume a different perspective with experience. She said, "I will not be so hasty next time. I will spend a year getting to know the institution."

On some campuses, actions of new presidents, such as organizational restructuring or changes of personnel, can increase confidence in presidential judgment. On other campuses, identical actions can lead to major insecurity and instability. Because each campus has its own culture and cognitive biases, presidents should be cautious and not uncritically accept the advice of other presidents about how they should approach their job.

New presidents should act early in their tenures as they would like to be remembered later; they may not get a second chance to make a first impression. As Bensimon (1989b, pp. 10–11) has pointed out, "Presidents who, in the urgency of resolving critical problems, overlook consultative processes run the risk of not getting campus support or cooperation when the time comes to implement necessary changes."

Listen with Respect, Be Open to Influence

One of the most potent themes running through the ILP research is the added increment of influence that presidents develop through respectful listening. Willingness to be influenced was the single most frequently identified dimension used by constituents to assess their presidents. Ninety percent of all ILP participants mentioned it. All presidents seen by faculty as open to influence received good ratings by them; almost all presidents seen as not being subject to influence received low faculty ratings (Fujita, 1990).

Most ILP presidents portrayed themselves as listeners who were open to influence. But the perceptions of their constituents were often quite different. As one faculty member said about his president, "After a conversation, she would invariably say that what she had heard was helpful. And then she would take action opposite to what had been expressed, instead of saying to us first that she disagreed and then taking the action she thought she should take. It is double-dealing and dishonest." Constituents were quick to note differences between authentic presidential listening with a mind open to persuasion and superficial listening used to manipulate others.

To some extent, the reasons for listening may be related to cognitive complexity. In an ILP report, Bensimon (1990b) compared how presidents with different levels of cognitive complexity (as determined by their own statements and the perceptions of others) viewed and interacted with their campuses. Presidents with low complexity saw their campuses as unitary organizations having shared goals. They sought additional information in order to be informed and to confirm their sense of control. Presidents with high complexity saw their campuses as including many constituencies with different perceptions of reality. They sought additional information in order to perceive the campus as others saw it. Less complex presidents thought of themselves as good listeners and saw themselves as distant, tough, and decisive leaders whose role was to keep reminding others of the institution's mission; more complex presidents constantly reminded themselves of the need to listen to what people were saying and believed in face-to-face communication, even though it was time-consuming, in order to have people come to share values and principles. Bensimon (p. 81) concluded that "clearly, presidents in the two groups have different purposes for listening to constituents. Those in the high perceived complexity group listen for signs that let them know whether the campus is moving at the same pace they are. Presidents in the low perceived complexity group listen in order to be more effective decision makers."

Listening and consulting serve instrumental purposes by providing more information, increasing commitment through participation, and facilitating communication. And they serve important interpretive purposes as well. Academics often have a preference for consultation as a mode of decision making; listening is thus a symbol that a leader understands academic culture.

Faculty know that presidents are listening when presidential actions reflect faculty influence. Being subject to faculty influence is *not* the same as agreeing with all faculty requests, and indeed presidential leadership could be maintained or strengthened even as presidents rejected resolutions of their faculty senates. Presidents did this by demonstrating that, even though they may not have endorsed a specific recommendation, they remained accountable to the senate and respected its judgment. Lee (1991, p. 47) discovered in her study of senates and presidents that "the 'batting average' for faculty recommendations was less important here than the administration's practice of explaining why, on occasion, it could not accept the senate's recommendation, or why it felt some modification was necessary."

Listening respectfully did not compromise presidents' ability to act but strengthened it. When presidents provided clear explanations that exposed their intellectual processes to faculty scrutiny, they reinforced the collegial values of their institutions and in doing so, enhanced their own stature. At one institution, for example, when rejecting a senate action on the grounds that it might have an adverse effect on academic freedom, the president said, "Nothing is ever final in a university. I have an open mind about [the resolution]. It's a discussion I'm prepared to engage in." The faculty senate chair remarked that the president rarely vetoed senate actions, but "if he does, he first comes back and tells us why and opens the door for further discussion." The president's veto was accepted even by those who opposed his action; the incident led faculty to see the president as principled, a supporter of important values such as academic freedom, and someone who took faculty actions seriously enough to engage in continuing dialogue with an open mind.

Those who wish to be exemplary presidents should never justify their actions solely on the basis of the authority of their office. They should explain their actions, and make themselves accountable for their behavior.

Find a Balance for Governance

Presidents are likely to find that the governance systems of their new campuses differ in many important ways from those of their previous institutions. They may be tempted to initiate change because the new, being unfamiliar, may also be thought of as wrong.

Governance systems evolve as unique reflections of institutional history, values, and accidental interactions. Even when structures look superficially similar, they are likely to reflect quite different interpretations of academic norms and understandings of what is right and proper. Governance systems are more than just structures for getting campus work done; they also certify status for participants, symbolize campus authority relationships, and focus attention on certain issues (Birnbaum, 1989b). Governance systems are manifestations of culture, and presidents run great risks when they attempt to change these systems before understanding both the instrumental and the interpretive roles systems play in institutional life. Presidents in the ILP who supported and worked with the existing faculty governance structures were likely to enjoy greater faculty support than presidents who opposed or circumvented them.

In dealing with governance, the best course of action is often to move deliberately, recognizing that the self-correcting properties of academic organizations will automatically set restorative responses in motion when the change sought is more than marginal. This is true not only for presidents who may attempt to weaken faculty governance, but for those who attempt to strengthen it as well. One president described how initial actions led to later difficulty: "I overly emphasized participatory democracy. I followed a person there who was extremely authoritarian. I created structures with lots of layers for decision making. People began to feel that the faculty senate had a lot of power. And their expectations became unrealistic — they expected me to check all decisions with them. I overdid a good thing. I finally told them I felt it was inefficient, and it was undermining the vice presidents, so now I try to stay in the middle."

Presidents may be more successful in changing governance patterns through symbolic acts which show that they understand how faculty interpret institutional life. For example, one president told how shortly after her appointment, she tried to overcome organizational gridlock. Rules and regulations were stifling creativity and innovation, she said, and so "I held an all-employee meeting, and at that meeting I took the governance manual, and I threw it in the trash can in front of them, on the stage. People were stunned. There was a faculty cheer that went up when I did it. You need a dramatic action to symbolize a new order." This president not only showed that she understood how faculty felt about the old way but also made extremely clear that in her eyes, too, it was blocking progress.

No specific governance pattern among ILP institutions proved to be associated with presidential success. Some presidents were praised for making faculty partners in decision making. Other presidents were praised for making decisions on their own after listening to faculty voices and consulting. However, four principles seemed widely important.

First, faculty support of the president depends on their belief that they have influence in governance. Second, influence in governance can come in at least two forms — through participation and through accountability. Third, good governance depends on acceptance, and to be acceptable, it must conform to the expectations of the participants. Fourth, understanding those expectations requires authentic listening and a sensitivity to the interpretive importance of governance structures and processes in academic settings.

Avoid Simple Thinking

Although the relationship between leaders' cognitive complexity and their leadership effectiveness has been studied in business organizations, prior to the ILP, it had not been considered in studying higher education. A summary of the research on complexity in nonacademic settings (Van der Veer, 1991) reports that, compared to executives seen as less complex, the ones seen to possess cognitive complexity take less time to solve problems, make better use of information, have better analytical skills, make fewer errors, are less affected by overload, and are more tolerant of uncertainty and more open to disconfirming evidence. In general, they have different leadership styles and are more effective managers. Cognitively complex people are believed to be particularly effective in complex environments and to perform better in areas involving planning, strategy, and analytical skills (Streufert and Swezey, 1986).

Much of what people in colleges and universities do — whether or not they hold leadership roles — is routine. But presidents are more likely than others to confront situations of great ambiguity and incomplete information. Cognitively complex people are more effective in complex environments, and high constituency support was related to leaders' high cognitive complexity.

Failed presidents almost uniformly had a linear view of leadership; under pressure, they acted expediently and took unilateral action to respond to what they perceived as a threatening environment. They saw few alternatives to the courses of action they followed, and believed that they had no choice in what they did.

In contrast, since environments themselves are not "givens" but are socially constructed (Weick, 1979), more complex presidents were able to respond to similar problems with a fair-sized repertoire of behaviors and approaches. Less complex presidents, for example, tended to respond to financial crisis by reducing staff or salaries; more complex presidents considered alternative strategies that included taking risks on new projects which publicly signified faith in the future or reinterpreting the institution's mission to develop pride in doing more with less.

The most successful ILP presidents were able to balance a number of potentially conflicting ideas in their behaviors. For example, they were seen as supporting faculty governance but exercising administrative prerogatives, as exemplifying institutional culture but moving their colleges in new directions, as being intensely involved in all aspects of the organization but not micromanaging, as celebrating institutional strengths while being sensitive to institutional weaknesses, and as being predictable while creating or supporting new initiatives. Exemplary presidents saw patterns, analyzed problems at a deep level, understood nuances, and were concerned about receiving feedback. In contrast, failed presidents tended to focus on specific problems, acted immediately, were insensitive to moral issues, and isolated themselves from feedback.

Presidents may increase their cognitive complexity by being frequently presented with evidence of the existence of multiple dimensions (Streufert and Swezey, 1986). Presidents may produce such evidence by consulting broadly enough to permit the emergence of multiple views, remaining open to evidence that disconfirms their own predilections, and actively seeking, rather than merely passively receiving, information about campus functioning. The use of administrative teams whose members fulfill different cognitive functions (Neumann, 1991c), or even regular consultation with colleagues who see the organization from different perspectives, may serve as an organizational analog to, or partial substitute for, cognitive complexity in an individual.

Presidents must have self-confidence, but at the same time make a conscious effort to continually challenge their experience and their conclusions. As presidents become experienced in a system, it is easy for them to reduce the questioning stance with which they entered and thus to simplify rather than complicate their understanding of their institutions.

Don't Emphasize the Bureaucratic Frame or Linear Strategies

Presidents who rely on the bureaucratic frame and linear strategies are less likely than others to enjoy constituent support and therefore less able to influence the interpretive life of their institutions. Presidents who depend on these relatively simple ways of thinking about leadership may often find themselves justifying their actions by saying, "Given the circumstances, I really had no choice."

When presidents overemphasize the bureaucratic frame, followers may be unable to see the president from other perspectives — collegial, political, or symbolic (Bensimon, 1990b). Being observed as bureaucratic makes it particularly difficult for the president to influence the symbolic life of the campus. This poses a particular problem for presidents of public institutions in an era of state mandates, budget reductions, and accountability. The external pressure on presidents to be more structural in order to conform to rational myths of campus effectiveness (Meyer and Rowan, 1983) may, ironically, reduce presidential influence by diminishing their ability to manage symbols and meaning.

Presidents who emphasize structure and analysis may be seen by the faculty as insensitive to academic values and preoccupied with means rather than ends. They alienate others as they attempt to influence them using the president's legal authority, or the president's ability to reward or punish. Presidents who emphasize a bureaucratic approach may find that it becomes self-perpetuating, as those subject to a president's unilateral actions come to expect this approach. When no opportunities are provided for faculty to develop experience in self-government and internal regulation, it is difficult for them to come to constructively participate in processes of shared authority. An ILP president who had made a number of top-down decisions upon his appointment found how difficult it was to change this approach when he wanted more faculty involvement in the operation of the institution. He reported, "I would not have said that three years ago because of the crisis we were in. At that time there was no room for democracy. Now we have made changes, and I would love to see the faculty play a more active role in a timely manner. But this is a problem, because they are not accustomed to assuming that role, and we do not have the time it sometimes takes them to reach closure on issues."

Similar problems are experienced by presidents who give too much attention to linear and adaptive strategies. They may lose sight of ends as they pursue means and allow institutional efficiency and survival to become goals in themselves.

Linear or adaptive strategies are not always inappropriate, but if they become habitual, they can deny meaning to institutional participants who no longer are able to answer the critical question of legitimacy, "Why are we together?" (Chaffee, 1984, p. 222). Even under significant financial pressure, presidents have a choice of how they will present the news of hard times to constituents. They can focus on the problems of the present, emphasize statistics and financial indicators, and let the data speak for themselves. Or they can present the information in the context of institutional stories about the past and the future and provide interpretation of its meaning. In her ILP study, Neumann (in press) has shown that when presidents provide that interpretation, faculty are more likely to maintain confidence both in their own efficacy and in their president's competence.

Emphasize Strong Values

Leadership is ultimately a moral act, because it involves interpretations of what an institution *should* do. Effective presidents act with a moral foundation that permits them to retain their equilibrium even as they are being buffeted by events. Good leaders do not try to create new values, but recognize that since organizations and their values can decay, one of their most important tasks is to reinforce or develop processes that constantly work to regenerate an institution's values (Gardner, 1990). Values permit principled and consistent action, even in the midst of uncertainty. They also permit leaders to be comfortable with the decisions they make. As one ILP president said, "It was a major realization that you sit on a razor blade and that you will get cut any way you move. So why not be virtuous and move your own way? The issue is not to be a politician but to have more integrity."

An overemphasis on survival can lead administrators to compromise values, cause faculty to question the purposes that undergird decisions, and reduce a president's capacity to influence interpretations. On one campus that had become preoccupied with student credit hours and budget constraints, faculty commented on the "budget-line mentality," and questioned whether the president supported certain programs because of their money-making potential, rather than because they were consistent with the mission of the institution. As a consequence, said one faculty member, "Morale is diminishing. The faculty feel that their work is not valued when they have to plead or plot for the minor support they have traditionally received. It makes the job twice as hard. It leads to a feeling that the administration are bottom-line people. The faculty resent the use of Harvard B[usiness] School terminology. We can't 'interface' everything, and we can't 'bottom-line' everything. We are trying to quantify results that just can't be quantified. The teacher-learner relationship is not valued as much as I would like."

When presidents are motivated by strong and consistent values, they are likely to influence others in their institutions to focus on these values as well. Values infuse presidents' behavior with meaning, provide legitimacy for their actions, and set a moral tone to their behavior. At an ILP college serving a minority population, for example, the president emphasized its historic mission and honored its past. One constituent said about the president, "The man dreams about opportunities for higher education for minorities. Wherever he is today, right now, that is probably what he is thinking about. Our president is working very hard on his dream." Constituents saw the campus as more than just a college; it was a community tied together by a special shared sense of purpose. The president's obvious dedication to the single most important value held on campus gave him extraordinary influence. Past, present, and future could all be linked, for example, as they were when he supported a new program initiative by relating it to "the noble vision of the founders."

Leadership involves value choices, and leaders can justify their actions at three different levels of moral judgment (Hodgkinson, 1991). At the first, and most primitive, level, leaders can be self-justifying and consider an action to be right because it is consistent with their own personal preferences. At the second, and higher, level, leaders can justify their actions as consistent with the values of a specific reference group. At the highest level of morality, a value is justified because it is consistent with principles and commitments. The ILP did not focus attention on the study of values, so judgments about their consequences are based more on scattered impressions than data. Nevertheless, faculty support appeared to be lowest for presidents whose principal concern was self-interest and the maintenance of their positions, rationales that were inherently self-justifying. Support was intermediate for presidents concerned with institutional interests such as growth in resources or prestige, second-level values that enjoyed institutional consensus. Support was highest for presidents who appeared committed to transcendent third-level values for which their institutions could serve as vehicles. These transcendent values varied; they might involve meeting the needs of a specific community, furthering the growth and development of individual learners, or creating knowledge. Many such transcendent themes were possible, and when they spoke fervently to shared campus beliefs, they could be potent mediators of president-constituent relationships. They also strengthened the president's status, because constituents evaluate a leader's effectiveness not only on perceived accomplishments but on perceived motivation as well (Hollander, 1987).

Values can be implicit in what a leader does, but in a symbolic environment, actions don't always speak louder than words. A faculty leader said of his new, well thought of, and principled president, "One thing that we lack in our new president is that we would like strong statements of principles as opposed to just inferring them . . . publicly and before the faculty." Public articulation of shared values engenders others' trust, and trust induces an increased openness to influence.

Focus on Strengths

Effective presidents emphasize, as much as they can, their colleges' strengths and see their faculty and administrative colleagues as a fundamental institutional resource. Less effective

leaders concentrate on their schools' weaknesses. They see their
job as correcting problems, and they often treat their colleagues
as the problems to be corrected. Talking to a campus constituent about a president for even a quarter of an hour will often
indicate if the president's focus is on strength or weakness. When
a president emphasizes weakness, the president's daily behavior
can be a steady and dispiriting reminder to everyone of defects,
crisis, and faultfinding. A president's focus on strength can constantly reaffirm that things are good and getting better, and that
working even harder in the common cause will be an exciting
and joyous adventure.

At one impoverished ILP institution, faculty morale remained high even as its limited resources came under increased
stress. The president explained that "they recognize that the administration is doing all it can do to support what the faculty
are all about." Faculty members made this recognition clear,
and said, "We have the feeling that we count. She has our interests at heart; her heart, time, and efforts are devoted to this
college. She recognizes people for their contribution. She tells
us that we are good teachers and we like to hear that. She gives
us a lot of stroking; it feels good, she loses no opportunity just
to say it."

The president's "stroking" was both genuine and adroit,
and appreciated on both counts. At another ILP institution, a
faculty leader enthusiastically commented about his college's new
president: "The difference is his attitude about faculty. He acts
as if faculty know what we're doing. He respects our opinion.
When he asks for input he listens and takes it into account. The
last two presidents gave the impression that if the faculty were
any good at all they'd be teaching somewhere else."

Encourage Leadership by Others

Leadership is not the act of one person, but, as the ILP data
show clearly, something distributed throughout an institution.
This means that presidents concerned with advancing their own
agenda must be responsive to the agendas of others as well. If
they are not, their constituents may make themselves less open

to influence, disengage—subtly or baldly—from interaction with the president, and pursue their individual interests. One faculty leader talked about the discouraging response he received when broaching an academic issue with an unresponsive president: "He didn't appear to be too interested. I felt demoralized and deflated. It is as though people just want to get lost here. I have also approached the president about the overall quality of the campus. I didn't get much of a response on that either."

The sharing of leadership does more than merely increase presidential influence. When leadership is shared, a college has multiple ways of sensing environmental change, checking for problems, and monitoring campus performance. Shared leadership is likely to provide a college with more complex ways of thinking. At the same time, it places a greater burden on the president to nurture the interpretive mechanisms that lead toward cognitive integration. It is likely that as environmental complexity increases, the usefulness of multiple leadership increases as well.

Presidents can sustain or help the development of multiple leadership by encouraging and rewarding participation in institutional processes, collecting and disseminating data of interest to constituencies, providing forums for constituencies to talk together, and promoting a campus climate of openness. Presidents who are in communication with various campus constituencies will be more likely to learn about any informal leaders with unusual campus influence and to understand how networks of influential people can be established to help make things happen.

In addition, there are specific things presidents might do to make participation by others, particularly faculty and trustees, more useful.

Improving Faculty Leadership

On most ILP campuses, faculty, administrators, or both criticized faculty leadership. The criticism was particularly pointed for faculty senates. There were complaints that too few faculty were involved, and not always the most able. In the words of one president, faculty leadership did not represent "the best and the brightest of the faculty. It is made up of those who love the intrigue of faculty governance, who are politically active."

Some of the criticism may stem from differences in the meaning of faculty leadership. One of Neumann's (1991b) ILP studies found that presidents tended to think of the good faculty leader as focusing attention on academic matters — teaching, scholarship, and research — while faculty officers more often conceived of good faculty leadership in terms of paying attention to faculty welfare, rights, and participation in governance. This difference in opinion was evident in some two-thirds of the institutions in the ILP sample. Having such differences, and being unaware of them, can lead to conflict and misinterpretation. Presidents who see good faculty leaders as good academics may see leaders who emphasize faculty rights as ineffective, self-serving, and unrepresentative.

But there is surely some truth in the notion that the best faculty do not participate. When senates are viewed as illegitimate by many on campus (because they are controlled by administrators, for example), faculty do not find a role in leadership attractive (Lee, 1991). There are few rewards for faculty participation in institutional governance, and on some campuses, those accepting leadership positions are actually disadvantaged. Senate presidents do not usually receive any conspicuous campus adulation. What is likely to increase faculty interest in participation? ILP data suggest three answers.

First, presidents should ensure that those in faculty leadership roles are accorded appropriate recognition by the administration and that actions of the senate are treated with the respect they deserve. At one ILP campus, the makeup of senate membership changed dramatically after a new president made senate consultation an integral part of institutional policy development. One faculty leader said, "Under the previous administration, the faculty executive committee was not taken seriously because the administration did not talk to the faculty. Now it is taken more seriously, so that the people who are elected to it have been upgraded to professors who wield a lot of power in their schools. Before it was the most dissatisfied, who could scream the loudest." As the role and importance of a senate become clearer, able senior people often become more inclined to participate in it.

Second, leadership as an interactive process is facilitated by the development of many different kinds of communication networks and opportunities to meet and talk. Senates may elect more constructive leaders if these leaders are given the opportunity to sit with the president's cabinet and to meet formally and informally with other influential people on campus. At several ILP campuses, faculty leaders sat on presidential cabinets. At one campus, the faculty executive committee met annually with the board and administration. Such interaction helps campus participants come to a greater consensus about the nature of reality and of college life. It can also contribute to more acceptable decisions because senate actions are less likely to be rejected when senate leaders participate in administrative cabinets (Lee, 1991).

Third, colleges can enhance the continuity of faculty leadership. Administrators generally come to their administrative positions with prior experience and the expectation that their new positions are more than short term. Faculty who fill formal leadership roles, however, usually have neither advantage. Since it often takes time for effective leaders to develop their skills through experience, senate or union heads who serve one-year terms — probably the most normal practice — will ordinarily have a difficult time providing leadership. Institutions in the ILP, in general, did not provide information, advice, or training to incoming faculty officers (Lee, 1991). Inordinate time is required for them to learn the structural and political terrain they must navigate; gaining more sophisticated insights only comes later.

Several of the institutions in the ILP had made an effort to improve this situation. One of the most intriguing devices provided for faculty leadership was a triumvirate consisting of the senate's president, president-elect, and former president. Originally started as a chance response to a need to consult with faculty during the summer when the senate wasn't in session, this system developed into an accepted practice in which the president routinely meets with "The Gang of Three." This was one of the few instances in which an institution made use of the experience of the past senate chair.

Improving Board Leadership

Private and public boards were generally considered by ILP presidents to fulfill different functions. Private boards were seen as supporters of the institution whose actions could strengthen presidential leadership. Public boards were often viewed as watchdogs and defenders of "the public interest." They were more likely to get involved in day-to-day operations and establish private communications with faculty and administrators.

Research into leadership by boards (Taylor, Chait, and Holland, 1991, p. 219) has found that, among private colleges, board effectiveness was related to board members' motivation. Members of effective boards joined because they had affection for the institution and supported its goals and values. They found satisfaction in helping their college develop and in seeking input from constituents. Members of ineffective boards joined because they saw the college as an instrument for achieving extrinsic goals. They found satisfaction in tangible measures of growth such as new buildings, and they tended to isolate themselves from constituencies and "to view faculty and students as adversaries to be outwitted and outmaneuvered."

This difference between effective and ineffective boards suggests that trustees may improve their effectiveness if they understand and support the key beliefs and values of their college and share a common view of reality with the president and their fellow board members. Achievement of this goal is more likely in the private than the public sector, because private boards are usually able to select their own members. In contrast, trustee selection in the public sector is usually a political process, and often a partisan one.

There may be little or nothing of substance that presidents can do to improve the selection process for trustees of public colleges. However, they might make their boards marginally more effective by balancing their agendas with interpretive as well as instrumental items. Boards can better come to understand the informal norms of their institution if they tour its campus, meet with its constituents, and participate in its nonacademic activities. New members should be introduced to a col-

lege's stories, heros, and sagas, as well as its budgets, procedures, and regulations. A number of ways of doing this have
been proposed (Chait, Holland, and Taylor, 1991), to give trustees a sense of institutional history and tradition.

Making sure that a board pays sufficient attention to
values and beliefs may prove difficult in multicampus systems,
which are often so complex and dispersed that trustees cannot
discover the subtleties of individual institutions. Such boards
become distant auditors, perhaps accounting for the ILP's finding
that these huge systems appear to inhibit the development of
campus leadership.

Check Your Own Performance

It is very difficult for people in colleges to obtain accurate feedback about their own performance and effectiveness. The difficulty of finding and interpreting data, a conflict between the
desire to know and the potential costs to the ego, and a concern
to avoid appearing weak or insecure are typical problems (Ashford, 1989) that may inhibit college presidents. And it probably does not help that most presidents believe they are more
effective than average and responsible for major institutional
improvements. Presidents build self-portraits of effectiveness
based on real or imagined successes. When faced with ambiguous situations, they are likely to anticipate — and therefore to
observe — successful outcomes and to attribute these to their own
efforts (Meindl, Ehrlich, and Dukerich, 1985; Birnbaum, 1986).

Some ILP presidents surrounded themselves with supporters who insulated them from the realities of campus disen-
chantment. Others, through their autocratic behavior, inhibited
accurate communication from campus constituents. While some
presidents discovered that it was important to listen and accept
criticism, others opted to tough things out and became insensitive to it. One ILP president discounted criticism as "part of
the territory. I look at it as part of my job. We are never going
to be crisis free." Some took the absence of criticism or simply
their length of service as proxies for success. One president assumed he was effective, because he heard "very little comment

to the contrary." Another long-term president said, "I seem now, during the last year or so, to have entered a period where the weight of a long period of office is becoming a positive factor in itself. I think people are saying 'if he has survived this long, he must be doing something right.'"

Of the thirty-two ILP presidents, a majority assessed themselves by considering their institution's performance; they said, "Effectiveness is ultimately measured by results." A smaller number gave weight to constituent satisfaction, believing that "the ultimate test is what other people think [about what you are doing]." Colleges were more often viewed by researchers and by faculty as improved when presidents used *both* outcomes and constituent feelings to assess their performance. Institutions were also more likely to be seen as improved when presidents engaged in an active search for information about their performance through campus tours, management by walking around, and informal meetings of various kinds, than when they relied on passive communications through meetings and other formal interactions.

The instrumental benefits of greater accuracy in self-assessment are unclear. It is possible that training and socialization produce presidents whose sensitivity to feedback, although flawed, is good enough, and that within the range of experiences presidents are likely to encounter, more accurate self-assessment may not markedly affect their performance or organizational outcomes (Birnbaum, 1990a). However, from an interpretive perspective, activities that make presidents more visible on campus, indicate their interest in receiving feedback, and provide greater opportunities for interaction may have positive consequences themselves, regardless of the nature of the information collected or the use to which it is put.

Know When to Leave

Campus leadership positions are roles and not careers. Presidents should be prepared to leave when they no longer have the support they need. The very act of leaving will probably activate the cycle of succession that permits institutions to periodically adjust their activities, structures, and sense of reality and provides them with needed, if temporary, freshness and excitement.

It is easy to advise presidents that it may be in their institution's best interests to leave voluntarily. The actual decision to leave is more difficult. The presidency is for many the culmination of a career. In most colleges it is the position of highest status and compensation. College presidents are not immune from American values that prize accomplishment and view positions achieved through competence, dedication, and hard work as prizes, well earned and worth protecting. Failed presidents, whose departure would help most, are also the most likely to exaggerate their importance, to believe incorrectly that they are venerated, and to seal themselves off from all evidence to the contrary. Modal presidents indulge less in self-deception but are still subject to unconscious biases that associate them with a college's successes and separate them from its failures. Moreover, their institutions function reasonably well, and there are few signs to say something is wrong. In fact, they are not bad presidents — they are just no longer able to provide renewing leadership because they have lost the ability to influence their faculty colleagues.

Most presidents provide the greatest benefit to their colleges at two points in their careers: when they arrive, and when they leave. If leave-taking is to be made more acceptable, at least two things need to happen. First, there must be an opportunity for honorable exits. This could be provided if presidents were appointed with tenure in a faculty position, with the right to revert to faculty status but to maintain their salary, perhaps not receiving increases until it was in line with other salaries. To be sure, this would be costly, but almost certainly it would be in the institution's long-term best interests.

Second, there must be cues available that permit presidents to obtain collective evidence of the level of their support. The need for departure could be made more obvious and, again, even more palatable if presidents, although serving at the pleasure of the board, were appointed to terms of stated length with reappointment subject to a process of review which would include an analysis of constituent support. Presidents should be expendable. The ultimate goal should be institutional improvement, not presidential survival. The purpose of such a review would not be to consider whether a president's reappointment was "fair," but whether it served institutional interests. Recent concerns about limited presidential terms may be misplaced. This is nothing inherently beneficial about long presidential terms, and on average, institutions might be better off with shorter rather than longer presidential tenures.

Summing Up

I estimated earlier that perhaps a quarter of college presidents will follow the path of the exemplary president; a quarter, that of failed president; and half, that of modal president. Although it would, of course, be desirable to increase the proportion of exemplary presidents, our knowledge of leadership in organizations is still too limited to suggest how this might be done. As we have seen, calls for more charismatic, transformational presidents are exercises in rhetoric, rather than responsible proposals for improvement. Charismatic leadership can be effective in the short run, but it is rare because no one knows how to do the magic. In the long run, it can weaken institutions by limiting, rather than empowering, leadership at lower levels.

We can have more confidence, however, in a suggestion for modal presidents; they can avoid failing if they avoid precipitate action without consultation and overcome the tendency to create self-sealing cycles of self-perceived effectiveness. Presidents lose effectiveness when they cease being learners and start being teachers. They increase their effectiveness when their behavior is grounded both in the values of their followers and in transcendental principles such as the development of human potential. It is through the mutual influence of leaders and followers that "the quality of leadership is functionally related to the moral climate of the organization and this, in turn, to the moral complexity and skills of the leader" (Hodgkinson, 1991, p. 129).

Presidents may be important in some situations, but the performance of colleges may usually be less dependent upon presidential leadership than most of us care to believe. Most college presidents do the right things, and do things right, most of the time. It is possible that college leaders can become marginally more effective. But those who seek major changes in the way presidents behave, or believe that such changes will make major differences on our campuses, are likely to be disappointed.

There are no quick fixes or magic bullets for presidential leadership in higher education. Ten-minute managers, pop psychologists, or charismatics with fixed ideas about what it takes to be a good college president need not apply. Good presidents come to their positions with useful competencies, integrity, faith in their colleagues, and a firm belief that by listening carefully and working together they can all do well. In a turbulent and undertain world, what happens after that is as much in the laps of the gods as in the hands of the president.

Institutions Participating in the Institutional Leadership Project

Universities

Arizona State University	Arizona
University of Denver	Colorado
Idaho State University	Idaho
Northwestern University	Illinois
Johns Hopkins University	Maryland
University of Missouri, Columbia	Missouri
Oregon State University	Oregon
Marquette University	Wisconsin

State Colleges

San Diego State University	California
Florida A & M University	Florida
Central Michigan University	Michigan
Kean College of New Jersey	New Jersey
New Mexico Highlands University	New Mexico
Fayetteville State University	North Carolina
Longwood College	Virginia
University of Wisconsin, Parkside	Wisconsin

Independent Colleges

Oglethorpe University	Georgia
Drake University	Iowa

Loyola University, New Orleans   Louisiana
Gordon College   Massachusetts
Smith College   Massachusetts
Rider College   New Jersey
Wilberforce University   Ohio
Saint Edward's University   Texas

Community Colleges

Santa Monica College   California
Bay de Noc Community College   Michigan
Crowder College   Missouri
Queensborough Community
    College of the City University
    of New York   New York
Sinclair Community College   Ohio
Piedmont Virginia Community
    College   Virginia
North Seattle Community College   Washington
West Virginia Northern
    Community College   West Virginia

RESOURCE B

Interview Protocol for "Old" Presidents

Initial Interview
(Two hours at beginning of visit)

Background

1. When were you appointed as president?
2. What was your position before that?
3. How were you selected for this position? (If search committee, probe for committee membership, process.)
4. There probably were a number of people who could have been considered for the presidency. What do you think are the most important reasons why you were selected?
5. Who preceded you in the position? In what ways would you describe yourself as similar to or as different from your predecessor?

Goals and Values

1. When you are asked to briefly describe (college), what do you say? What do you think is really important around here?
2. What are the major goals of (college)?
3. In what ways do you hope the college will be different five years from now than it is today?

Taking Charge

1. We are interested in learning about what leaders do when they first take over their new positions. What were your first impressions of (college) when you took office?
2. What were the most important problems or things you had to deal with immediately when you became president? Why did you think that these problems were so important? How did you deal with them? What were the outcomes for the college and for you?
3. To what institutional problems or areas do you give the most attention now?
4. If a colleague came to you and said, "I've just accepted the presidency of an institution very much like this one. Can you give me any advice about what I should do my first few months in office," what would you say?
5. What do you as president have to do to get things done around here?

Identifying Leaders

So far, we have been talking about the presidency. On most campuses, there are other people who have leadership roles as well. I'd like to ask you about these people.

1. Who do you think are some of the important leaders on this campus? Why do you consider them to be important leaders?
2. I'm interested in the ways in which people on campus work together. Could you describe your working relationship with the leaders you have mentioned? (Probe for board, faculty, administrative, and student leaders not mentioned.)
3. There has been a lot of talk lately about the need for good faculty leadership on college campuses. How would you describe "good faculty leadership"? How about good trustee leadership? How about good leadership among senior administrators other than the president?

Critical Incident

1. Sometimes it is easier to get a clearer picture about how a college works by discussing something very concrete. What do you think was the most important event or incident on campus during the past year or so?
2. Could you describe it in more detail? Who played leadership roles? What role did you play in it?

Leader Effectiveness

1. How would you describe yourself as a leader?
2. What do you think are the major effects you have had on this campus as president? Which of these has given you the greatest sense of accomplishment?
3. How do you tell if you are being effective as a leader?

The Future

1. What do you think will be the most important issue or problem on campus over the next year or so?
2. What leads you to say that? How are you likely to be involved in it? How is it likely to turn out?

Final Interview
(One hour at end of visit)

1. The term *leadership* is used all the time, but people don't always agree on what it means. What does the word *leadership* mean to you?
2. If people around here were asked to describe you as a leader, what do you think they would say?
3. Presidents are always subject to criticism of one kind or another. What criticisms of your leadership are you aware of?
4. Over what areas of campus life do you have the most influence? The least influence?
5. In what ways are your ideas about leadership different now than when you took office?

6. What would you consider the single biggest mistake you have made; if you had it to do all over again, what would you do differently?

7. What is the single event or incident that has had the greatest impact upon your presidency?

8. Some people say that presidents can provide the strongest leadership when they first take office. Others say that leadership is strengthened by a long tenure in office. During what part of your term did you feel you were able to exercise the strongest leadership?

9. When during your term did you first feel "in charge"?

10. Is there anything else you would like to say about leadership on this campus, or in higher education in general?

Supplementary
Research Data

This Resource presents three kinds of data that were used in developing some of the ideas in this book. The first section describes characteristics of the ILP institutions, the backgrounds and gender of their presidents, and the cognitive processes and patterns through which these presidents made sense of their institutions and their leadership roles. The second section describes the relationship between these characteristics and the level of faculty support that these presidents enjoyed. The third section relates these characteristics and faculty support levels to campus changes between the ILP interviews in 1986–87 and 1988–89.

Section One: Characteristics of Institutions, Presidents, and Cognitive Processes

Data describing institutional characteristics and the personal characteristics of presidents were compiled from interviews, observations, and documents such as annual reports, presidential résumés, institutional bulletins, and federal Higher Education General Information Survey (HEGIS) responses as analyzed by the National Center for Higher Education Management Systems (NCHEMS). The distribution of institutional characteristics is summarized in Table 1, and the distribution of personal characteristics is summarized in Table 2.

Table 1. Characteristics of ILP Institutions.

	Number of Institutions	Percent of Institutions
Institutional Type[a]		
University	8	25.0
State college	8	25.0
Independent college	8	25.0
Community college	8	25.0
Control Auspices[a]		
Public	20	62.5
Nonpublic	12	37.5
Faculty Union[a b]		
Yes	10	31.2
No	22	68.8
Part of System[a]		
Yes	11	34.4
No	21	65.6
Size in FTE Students		
Under 1,000	3	9.4
1,000 to 2,499	7	21.9
2,500 to 4,999	8	25.0
5,000 to 9,999	8	25.0
10,000 and higher	6	18.8
Wealth in E&G Expenditures per FTE Student		
$2,500 to $4,999	8	25.0
$5,000 to $9,999	17	53.1
$10,000 to $19,999	5	15.6
$20,000 and higher	2	6.3
Presence of Crisis		
Yes	8	25.0
No	24	75.0

[a]Distribution was determined by research design.

[b]Four state colleges and four community colleges were selected on the basis of faculty collective bargaining. Two independent colleges, by chance, also had faculty unions.

Table 2. Personal Characteristics of ILP Presidents.

	Number of Presidents	Percent of Presidents
Gender[a]		
Male	24	75.0
Female	8	25.0
Length of Tenure[a]		
(year appointed less 1986 base year)[b]		
New presidents[b]		
0–3 years	16	50.0
Old presidents[c]		
5–9 years	5	15.6
10–14 years	6	18.8
15–19 years	4	12.5
20–24 years	1	3.1
Faculty Experience		
Yes	23	71.9
No	9	28.1
Academic Vice President Experience		
Yes	18	56.3
No	13	40.6
Not known	1	3.1
Previous Presidencies		
None	26	81.3
One	5	15.6
Two	1	3.1
Selected From		
Outside institution	23	71.9
Inside institution	9	28.1

[a]Distribution was determined by research design.
[b]Average: 1.2 years, plus .5 year adjustment = 1.7 years.
[c]Average: 12.2 years, plus .5 years adjustment = 12.7 years

The ILP considered four aspects of the ways in which presidents think — analyzing their cognitive frames, cognitive complexity, strategy, and implicit leadership theories. The distribution of the thirty-two presidents in office during the time of the first campus visit in 1986–87 for each of these characteristics is described below. Each characteristic or process is briefly

defined in Chapter Three and is analyzed in greater detail in
the cited ILP publications.

Cognitive Frames

Based on their self-descriptions, Bensimon (1990b) categorized
seventeen (53 percent) of the ILP presidents as utilizing a bureaucratic frame; seventeen (53 percent), a collegial frame; fifteen
(47 percent), a political frame; and twenty-one (66 percent), a
symbolic frame. These numbers do not add up to thirty-two
or to 100 percent because a number of presidents used more
than one frame.

Cognitive Complexity

Bensimon (1989c) examined the cognitive complexity of ILP
presidents when they talked about leadership. Of the thirty-two
presidents in this study, thirteen (41 percent) described leadership using a single frame, eleven (34 percent) used two frames,
seven (22 percent) used three frames, and only one (3 percent)
identified all four frames. But Bensimon (1990b) found significant discrepancies between the frames presidents said they used
and the frames constituents saw them use. While 66 percent of
the presidents described leadership using the symbolic frame,
only 36 percent of other campus leaders included a symbolic
component when describing their presidents. There were also
major differences in the cognitive complexity of presidents as
they described themselves (avowed complexity) and as they were
described by their constituents (observed complexity). While
nineteen presidents (59 percent) avowed complexity that used
two or more frames, far fewer presidents were seen that way
by others. For the twenty-eight presidents for whom data were
available, eight (29 percent) had high observed complexity and
nine (32 percent) had low observed complexity. The other eleven
were of intermediate complexity. Presidents high in observed
complexity had a self-image that consisted of collegial, political, and symbolic qualities, and campus constituents agreed with
the presidential self-assessment. In contrast, presidents low in

observed complexity had a self-image that was primarily bureaucratic and symbolic, but they were not seen that way by their constituents. Although more than half the presidents with low observed complexity thought of themselves as using symbolic leadership behavior, only 9 percent of the other campus leaders agreed. Most saw these presidents as primarily bureaucratic, suggesting that when bureaucratic frames are used by less cognitively complex presidents they overwhelm any other presidential behavior. The perceptual congruence of presidents and their observers seems to be mediated by the bureaucratic frame, so that presidents who rely excessively on the bureaucratic frame are unlikely to be able to exercise collegial, political, or symbolic influence on campus.

Strategy

Neumann (1989b) analyzed the strategic orientations of the ILP presidents based on how presidents during the initial interview in 1986–87 described what they were doing and why they were doing it. Of the thirty-two ILP presidents, Neumann categorized fifteen (47 percent) as using linear strategy, seventeen (53 percent) as using adaptive strategy, and nineteen (59 percent) as using interpretive strategy. In addition, seventeen (53 percent) appeared to rely primarily on a single strategy, while fifteen (47 percent) used multiple strategies (that is, either two or three strategies in combination).

Implicit Leadership Theories

Birnbaum (1989c) analyzed the definitions of leadership given by ILP presidents to determine the theories implicit within them.

One- or Two-way Communication. Most presidents thought of leadership as a process of influence directed toward the achievement of goals. They differed, however, in describing how such goals were developed and communicated. Most of the presidents — twenty of the twenty-eight for whom data were available (71 percent) — described leadership as a process of one-way communication in which they, as president, were expected to influence others. Eight presidents (29 percent) identified the communications process as a two-way exchange in which leaders and their constituents interacted and mutually influenced each other.

Directive or Enabling Roles. Presidents were also more likely (22 of 28, or 79 percent) to describe the leader's role as directive than as enabling. The directive view was that leaders were responsible for determining the directions in which an institution should move and coordinating the structure and process to help it get there. Leadership was considered a manifestation of the behavior of an individual. The enabling view (six, or 21 percent) emphasized leadership as a group, rather than an individual, phenomenon. The role of a leader was not to direct the group but to facilitate the emergence of the pluralistic leadership latent within it.

Self-evaluation. College presidents function in complex and ambiguous environments that make accurate learning difficult. How do they evaluate their own performance? Birnbaum (1990a) analyzed how the thirty-two ILP presidents assessed their own effectiveness and discovered what was happening on their campuses.

Eighteen presidents (56 percent) indicated that they judged their effectiveness by looking at institutional performance. They believed that organizational effectiveness was measured by results, and that an effective institution implied an effective president. Three presidents (9 percent) emphasized the importance of constituent reactions and judged the positive comments and satisfaction of trustees, students, faculty, and other institutional constituents as a reflection of their own presidential performance. Eleven presidents (34 percent) indicated that they relied on both institutional performance and constituent reactions.

Passive or Active Search. Presidents found themselves flooded with information that came through formal structures and institutional processes as well as informal networks. For some presidents, however, receipt of information through passive means was not enough, and half of them (50 percent) said that they engaged in an active search for more. When presidents were asked how they constructed meanings from the information they received, half (50 percent) indicated that they relied on intuition. It was not clear whether the intuition of which they spoke was real or illusory — whether it was an almost instant cognitive process that permits experienced leaders to make judgments based on perceiving familiar patterns or merely a convenient way for befuddled presidents to give a socially acceptable response to justify what they could neither explain nor understand.

Section Two: Institutional Characteristics, Personal Characteristics and Cognitive Characteristics, and Constituent Support

Of the thirty-two ILP presidents in office in 1986–87, sixteen (50 percent) were judged as having high faculty support, seven (22 percent) as having mixed faculty support, and nine (28 percent) as having low support (Birnbaum, 1992).

Institutional Characteristics

Neither institutional category, institutional control, institutional size, nor the presence of a campus crisis appeared related to the level of faculty support enjoyed by a president. Several institutional characteristics — including unionization, system membership, and wealth — did appear to make a difference, however. Faculty in unionized institutions were more likely to rate their president as poor (50 percent) than faculty in nonunionized institutions (18 percent). Faculty in institutions that were part of systems were more likely to rate their presidents as poor (46 percent) than were faculty in nonsystem institutions (19 percent). And faculty in institutions with moderate expenditures per student were more likely to give low ratings to their presidents (41 percent), than were faculty in either poorer institutions (12 percent) or richer institutions (14 percent).

Personal Characteristics

ILP presidents came to their roles with different characteristics, professional backgrounds, and experiences. Most of these — such as whether a president was male or female, had been chosen from inside or outside the institution, had previous presidential experience, or had ever been a faculty member or chief academic officer — were unrelated to faculty ratings. However, as shown in Table 3, one factor that was highly related to faculty support was whether a president was new or old. Seventy-five percent of new presidents (with an average tenure of 1.7 years) enjoyed high faculty support, compared to only 25 percent of old presidents (with an average tenure of 12.7 years).

Cognitive Characteristics

Several cognitive characteristics were related to levels of faculty support.

Cognitive Frames. The greater the president's cognitive complexity, as reflected by perceptions by others that the president's behavior reflected the use of multiple frames, the more likely the president was to be highly rated by the faculty. Two of ten (20 percent) of presidents with low complexity, six of eleven (55 percent) with moderate complexity, and six of eight (75 percent) with high complexity enjoyed high faculty support.

Strategy. Those presidents who self-reported an orientation to leadership that included the use of linear strategy were less likely to be highly rated by faculty (five of fifteen, or 33 percent) than those who did not (eleven of seventeen, or 65 percent). Self-reports of using adaptive or interpretive strategy were unrelated to faculty support, but the use of multiple strategies showed a

Table 3. Faculty Support of "New" and "Old" Presidents.

| President Category | Level of Faculty Support | | |
	High	Mixed	Low
New president (n = 16)	12	2	2
Old president (n = 16)	4	5	7
Total	16	7	9

strong relationship. Of the seventeen presidents who used multiple strategies, only six (35 percent) were highly rated by their faculty. This compared to high ratings for ten of the fifteen (67 percent) who used only single strategies. However, not all single strategies had the same relationship to faculty assessments. The three presidents who used only linear strategies and the three using only adaptive strategies did not appear to have higher faculty support than their colleagues who used multiple strategies. In contrast, seven of the nine (78 percent) using interpretive strategies received high faculty ratings.

Implicit Leadership Theories. Faculty ratings of presidents were not related to whether presidents verbally endorsed one- or two-way communication, saw their roles as directive or enabling, assessed outcomes by looking at results or constituent feedback, or claimed to act intuitively. The absence of a relationship between communication patterns and faculty support is somewhat surprising, but it should be remembered that what presidents say they do may not always be a good indicator of how they actually behave.

Section Three: Leadership and Change

Understanding the effects of leadership on a campus might appear to involve a relatively simple process of identifying changes during the follow-up visit and relating them to constituent support or to presidential, institutional, and cognitive characteristics identified during the first visit. Following this procedure during a preliminary analysis led to results that were so contrary to conventional expectations that they were not credible. For example, some of the institutions with the lowest faculty support of the president during the first visit turned out to have the largest improvements on certain dimensions of campus functioning—for example, faculty morale—at the time of the second visit. This finding seemed highly implausible.

Once discovered, the reason for the apparent anomaly was obvious. The data were collected at two different times and originally analyzed with the tacit—and incorrect—assumption

that the same president was in office at both times. In fact, of
the thirty-two presidents visited in year one, seven (two new
and five old) had left their institutions by the second visit. In
addition, four presidents still in office (all old) had publicly announced the dates of their resignation as of the second visit.
Where presidents had left, campus changes seen in year two
might have been due to the actions of the replacement president rather than those of the original president. Moreover,
most of the presidents who left or were leaving did not have
strong faculty support, so that improvement in faculty morale
may have been due as much to the arrival or promise of a new
president as to any actions by either the old presidents or their
replacements.

The analysis of leadership and change, therefore, focuses
on the twenty-one stable campuses at which the same president
was in office during both visits. Occasional references will be
made as appropriate to the eleven transitional institutions at
which presidents either had left or announced their intention
to do so.

Reducing the number of institutions eliminates potential
confusion related to having more than one president, but at the
same time makes it even more difficult to see patterns in the
data; as numbers became smaller, changing the assessment at
even one institution could have major consequences. To partially compensate for the reduced number of institutions, the
analyses that follow are conservative, and (with several exceptions that are identified) only relationships that appear strong
and consistent are mentioned. Nevertheless, these relationships
should be considered as hypotheses deserving further consideration in future research, rather than as conclusions in which
great confidence can be expressed.

Changes Assessed by Researchers

There is a long tradition in which institutional performance is
evaluated by researchers who base their judgments of a college
on their observations, without necessarily employing any explicit criteria. The four ILP researchers who conducted the

follow-up visits in 1988–89 were all experienced administrators and scholars. They were asked to provide their global, comprehensive assessment of whether, all things considered, a campus appeared to be "better off" during the second visit than during the first.

Researchers made their judgments after reviewing documents and transcripts of interviews conducted during the first visit in 1987–88, and conducting an extended campus visit in 1988–89, during which they observed campus activity and interviewed campus leaders. They then prepared an extensive case analysis of the campus in which they summarized interviews in both years and analyzed perceptions of campus changes during the two-year period.

Researchers had access to a considerable amount of data, but no attempt was made to develop a common understanding of "better off." Therefore, no assertion is made that their ratings met any normative criterion of validity or reliability, or were based on anything other than their individual intuition and judgment. The ways in which they arrived at a general summative impression of the campus were probably similar to, and reflected both the strengths and weaknesses of, the processes by which campus observers and participants most frequently reach judgments and make sense of their institutions.

Of the twenty-one institutions with the same presidents, researchers believed that nine (43 percent) had improved, six (29 percent) remained unchanged, and six (29 percent) had worsened between the first and second visits. The distribution of researcher ratings of global institutional change for all thirty-two institutions is shown in Table 4.

Constituent Support. Researcher ratings were unrelated to constituent support. Institutions where continuing presidents enjoyed high faculty support in year one were no more likely than other campuses to be seen by researchers as having improved over the two-year period.

Institutional Characteristics. Institutional characteristics were not in general related to researcher ratings of campus change.

Table 4. Researcher Ratings of Changes in Overall
Campus Status Between 1987–88 and 1988–89.

Rating	Number of Institutions	Percent of Institutions
Much worse	2	6.3
Somewhat worse	6	18.8
Same or mixed	7	21.9
Somewhat better	12	37.5
Much better	5	15.6

The major exception was that institutions considered to be in crisis during the first visit, and having stable leadership, were more likely at the time of the second visit to be seen as having improved than institutions not in crisis. It is not clear whether crisis brings out certain presidential actions that help improve campus functioning, or whether crises always eventually abate regardless of presidential behavior, owing either to the actions of other campus constituencies, environmental changes, or merely the passage of time.

Personal Characteristics. There was only one noteworthy pattern relating personal characteristics and researcher assessments of campus change. Researchers were much more likely to see improvements at campuses with new presidents than with old presidents. They were also likely to rate campuses with presidents who had left or were leaving as having improved. These data suggest that most presidents may be seen as having a positive influence on their campuses at two times in their careers—when they arrive and when they leave.

Cognitive Characteristics. Two cognitive factors for stable presidents were related to researcher assessments. One was the process through which presidents assessed their own effectiveness. Presidents who stated that they assessed themselves by monitoring both institutional outcomes and constituent responses were more likely to have institutions that experts rated as improved than those who considered constituent responses only, or outcomes only.

The other cognitive factor was the self-report of presidential involvement in active searches for campus information. Researchers were much more likely to find improvement on campuses at which stable presidents had indicated that they engaged in both formal and informal active search processes, than on campuses at which they gave no indication of active search.

Changes Assessed by Faculty

Although leaders may not actually have the instrumental effects on campus life and performance that some claim, it is certainly true that they are often *believed* to have such effects. Perceived changes in institutional functioning are, therefore, often attributed to leadership, and the quality of leadership can be inferred from perceptions of changes in critical areas of institutional functioning.

Because roles filter perceptions, it is expected that at many institutions different groups — for example, trustees, administrators, or community leaders — will disagree on the extent to which an institution has changed in certain dimensions of functioning. Although the perceptions of any of these groups could legitimately be considered as reflecting important institutional change, this chapter uses the responses of faculty because they are the major providers of institutional services.

When faculty were interviewed in year two, they were explicitly asked for their perceptions of changes in four areas of institutional functioning between the first and second campus visits, as well as their assessments of overall campus change. The four areas included faculty perceptions of campus morale, financial condition, governance processes, and educational quality. Researchers coded interview responses as indicating faculty perceptions that things had improved, had remained the same or were mixed, or had worsened during the two-year period. The distribution of responses at the thirty-two institutions for each of the four areas and the faculty members' assessment of "general change" are shown in Table 5.

Most faculty saw their institutions as either improving or remaining constant in terms of morale, finances, governance, quality, and overall change during the two-year period. Faculty

Table 5. Faculty Perceptions of Changes in Critical Areas
of Institutional Performance Between 1986–87 and 1988–89.

| | Changes | | | | | |
| | Improved | | Same or Mixed | | Worsened | |
Performance Area	Number of faculties	Percent of faculties	Number of faculties	Percent of faculties	Number of faculties	Percent of faculties
Morale	15	46.9	9	28.1	8	25.0
Financial	7	21.9	15	46.9	10	31.3
Governance	11	34.4	19	59.4	2	6.3
Quality	15	46.9	16	50.0	1	3.1
General change	15	46.9	14	43.8	3	9.4

perceptions of general change were highly correlated with morale change, but unrelated to perceptions of other changes. The changes on each of five dimensions of campus functioning were summated and then categorized to identify institutions that were seen by the faculty as having improved, remained the same, or worsened over the previous two years.

Among the twenty-one institutions with the same presidents, faculty at four (19 percent) saw improvement in institutional effectiveness, nine (43 percent) believed the campus had remained the same, and faculty at eight (38 percent) rated it as worsening.

Constituent Support. There was no relationship between constituent support and faculty perceptions of institutional change.

Institutional Characteristics. There was only one institutional characteristic—the earlier presence of an institutional crisis—that appeared clearly related to faculty assessments of change. None of the institutions that had been identified in crisis at the time of the earlier visit, but half of those not in crisis at that time, were seen by faculty as having worsened.

Personal Characteristics. Presidential tenure was the most important personal factor affecting faculty perceptions of change. Faculty on campuses with old presidents were more likely to believe that the campus had worsened than were faculty on campuses with new presidents. Few campuses with stable presidents were seen as improved, while improvement was much more likely to be seen on campuses where presidents had left or were leaving, a finding consistent with data on researcher assessments reported earlier. There was also a tendency for faculty to see more changes for the worse when stable presidents had been selected from inside the institution rather than from outside.

Cognitive Characteristics. Only one cognitive characteristic — the president's method of self-assessment — appeared related to faculty perceptions of institutional change. Faculty on campuses at which presidents said they assessed their own performance by considering only institutional outcomes were more likely to see the campus as having worsened than those on campuses whose presidents indicated that they considered both outcomes and constituent satisfaction.

Consistency and Discrepancy in President-Faculty Perceptions

One of the major functions of leadership is to help organizational participants make sense of a dynamic and equivocal world and develop some common understandings about the nature of reality. The extent of agreement or disagreement between faculty and president on the nature of campus changes over the previous two years may therefore be a reflection of leadership.

Consistency in the assessments made by presidents and their faculties was determined by comparing both groups on the campus: change ratings described in the previous section. A comparison of the perceptions of change for all thirty-two institutions on one of these measures — general campus change — is shown in Table 6. That comparison shows that presidents were more likely to see their institutions improving (twenty-one of thirty-two, or 66 percent) than were faculty (fifteen of thirty-two, or 47 percent), reflecting the common cognitive bias that often induces leaders to have inflated views of their own effectiveness.

A discrepancy index was developed by adding together the absolute differences between presidential and faculty ratings

Table 6. Comparisons of Presidential and Faculty Assessments
of General Institutional Change Between 1986–87 and 1988–89.

| Presidents Say Institution Has: | Faculty Say Institution Has: | | | |
	Improved	Same or mixed	Worsened	Total
Improved	13	7	1	21
Same or mixed	1	6	0	7
Worsened	1	1	2	4
Total	15	14	3	32

for each of the five elements of campus change. Of the twenty-one campuses with stable presidents, there was no discrepancy in their judgments of campus change at five (24 percent) of the campuses, low discrepancy at eleven (52 percent), and high discrepancy at five (24 percent).

Constituent Support. Faculty support of the president was unrelated to consistency in their views of campus change.

Institutional Characteristics. No institutional characteristics were related to high discrepancies, but several appeared moderately related to having no discrepancy. Institutions without collective bargaining, not part of systems, or independent were somewhat more likely to have no discrepancy than bargaining institutions, system institutions, or community colleges.

Personal Characteristics. Several presidential characteristics were related to no discrepancies in faculty-president perceptions, although none were related to high discrepancies. Institutions were more likely to have no discrepancy when presidents had previously been a faculty member, when they had previously been a chief academic officer, or when they were male.

Cognitive Characteristics. Cognitive factors may have been mediators of discrepancies in faculty-president views of institutional improvement, but small numbers make analysis difficult. Presidents were slightly more likely to have campuses with high levels of discrepancy when their views of leadership stressed one-way rather than two-way communication, when their implicit theories emphasized directive rather than enabling leadership, and when they used linear strategy. Presidents were more likely to have campuses with no discrepancy when they engaged in active search and when they assessed themselves based on both outcomes and constituency satisfaction than when they relied solely on outcomes.

Institutional Stress

Stress is ubiquitous in organizational life. A certain level of stress is probably necessary if an institution is to be innovative and responsive to changing environments. But too high a level of stress can overwhelm organizational processes, threaten institutional values, and shatter systems of communication. One of the functions of leadership is to keep organizational stress within tolerable limits. Leaders can do this to the extent that they can either instrumentally influence the cause of stress or influence the way that potentially stressful situations are interpreted.

Researchers used data collected from each campus during the second visit to rate stress in each of four areas of institutional functioning. These four were selected as representing major areas of potential stress in institutional inputs (resource stress), processes (governance stress and stress caused by administrative succession), and outputs (productivity stress). Each of the four areas was rated on a five-point scale, on which 1 indicated no stress, 5 meant very high stress, and the middle rating of 3 reflected a moderate level of stress that would normally be expected in the type of institution being rated. The following specific definitions given for the ratings of resource stress are illustrative of the definitions used for the other stress factors as well.

1 *None:* Institution has significant slack resources and few unmet needs — is able to build reserves.
2 *Very Low:* Budgets are balanced and sufficient to meet institution's needs.

3 *Moderate:* Budgets are balanced, most programs are funded at levels that permit continued operation, but not all needs are met; priorities are established through expected budget and planning systems.

4 *High:* Budgets have minor imbalances, programs of lower priority are in jeopardy; budget processes are affected by unexpected political and administrative processes.

5 *Very High:* Budgets have major imbalances, major programs are in jeopardy and institutional integrity severely threatened; expected budget processes and systems inoperable.

Stress levels were determined based on the perceptions of campus participants as revealed in interviews, and not on "objective" analyses of financial or other data. The distribution of stress levels in each area for the thirty-two campuses is shown in Table 7.

The total stress level in an institution was determined by summing its four stress scores. While the total stress rating was highly correlated to each of its four components, only two of the six possible relationships between the component factors were related. Governance stress was significantly correlated both with succession stress and productivity stress. Of particular interest was that resource stress was not significantly related to the other stress factors and had the smallest correlation with total stress.

Nine (43 percent) of the twenty-one campuses with stable presidents were rated as having low stress, eight (38 percent) had moderate stress, and four (19 percent) were under high stress.

Constituent Support. Constituent support was not related to stress levels.

Institutional Characteristics. Institutions with a previous crisis were more likely to have moderate or high stress than institutions that had not been in crisis earlier.

Table 7. Researcher Assessment of Levels of Stress in Each of Four Areas of Institutional Functioning.

| | Source of Stress | | | | | | | |
| Level of Stress | Resource | | Governance | | Succession | | Productivity | |
	Number of institutions	Percent of institutions	Number of institutions	Percent of institutions	Number of institutions	Percent of institutions	Number of institutions	Percent of institutions
None (1)	2	6.3	2	6.3	8	25.0	1	3.1
Low (2)	6	18.8	11	34.4	10	31.3	11	34.4
Moderate (3)	12	37.5	8	25.0	4	12.5	13	40.6
High (4)	9	28.1	8	25.0	9	28.1	4	12.5
Very high (5)	3	9.4	3	9.4	1	3.1	3	9.4
Average	3.2		3.0		2.5		2.9	

Personal Characteristics. Old presidents were more likely than new presidents to be seen on campuses with low stress.

Cognitive Characteristics. Several possible relationships were found between cognitive characteristics and institutional stress, although the numbers were too small in some cases to make any interpretation with confidence. The campuses of presidents emphasizing one-way communication, having directive leadership theories, or assessing themselves based on campus outcomes, were slightly more likely to have either high or low stress than those of presidents stressing two-way communication, emphasizing enabling leadership, or assessing themselves using both outcomes and constituent satisfaction.

Campus stress was more likely to be high when presidents used linear or mixed strategies, and to be low when they used adaptive or interpretive strategies.

Changes in Resources

Through their roles as institutional representatives, presidents may affect student recruitment, acquisition of fiscal resources, or the development of external support. However, this influence is limited by a number of factors. Because the resources of most institutions are enrollment-related, resources may depend on changes in demography over which institutions have no control. In addition, in the public sector, and particularly among institutions that are part of state systems, fiscal support may be determined by formulas applicable to an entire class of institution, independent of the nature of presidential leadership. For both public and private colleges, external support through research grants or fund-raising campaigns is related to faculty quality and institutional reputations which tend to be stable over time and particularly difficult to change over the short run. However, although leadership-related changes in resources may be difficult to achieve, they are theoretically possible.

Resource change was defined as changes in total full-time equivalent (FTE) enrollment, and in educational and general (E&G) expenditures per FTE student in constant dollars for the period 1985–86 to 1988–89. For the thirty-two institutions in this study, the period was one of generally rising enrollments and E&G budget increases adjusted for inflation. FTE enrollments increased 6 percent on average, ranging from a decrease of 14 percent to an increase of 50 percent. In all, twenty-four institutions maintained or increased their FTE enrollment, while eight decreased. E&G budget expenses per FTE student increased an average of 20 percent (7 percentage points over the Higher Education Price Index — HEPI), with 1988–89 expenditures ranging from 0.88 to 1.74 percent of their 1986–89 values. Of the thirty-two institutions, nine saw these expenditures change at a rate lower than inflation, and twenty-three saw them increase at a rate equal to or in excess of inflation.

Unfortunately, neither enrollment changes nor E&G expenditure levels by themselves give an accurate picture of institutional resources, and it is not possible to add these two measurements to develop a single scale of resource acquisition. In this study, for example, enrollment increases were not always accompanied by a concomitant increase in funding, and large (and apparently desirable) increases in FTE funding per student were caused in some cases by enrollment declines. In these cases, indicators that at first might have appeared to reflect a positive change would have been in actuality an indication of resource difficulty.

A measure of "total resource change" was developed to respond to this problem. Institutions were considered to have positive total resource change if they maintained or increased both their enrollments and their educational expenditures (in constant dollars) per FTE student. Institutions were considered to have negative total resource change if they failed one or both of these tests.

Of the twenty-one institutions with stable presidencies, eleven had negative resource change during the study period, and ten had positive resource change.

Constituent Support. There was no relationship between constituent support and total resource change.

Institutional Characteristics. A number of institutional characteristics appeared related to resource change. Bargaining institutions were more likely to have decreased resources than nonbar-
gaining; institutions in crisis were more likely to have decreased
resources than those not in crisis; state colleges were more likely
to lose resources than universities; and institutions with enrollments of one thousand to five thousand were more likely to suffer
resource reductions than larger institutions.

Personal Characteristics. Institutions whose presidents were selected from inside or had previously been faculty members were
more likely to experience negative resource change than those
whose presidents came from outside or had never had faculty
experience.

Cognitive Characteristics. Resources were more likely to decrease
in institutions whose presidents held implicit leadership theories
that supported one-way communication and directive leadership than in those where presidents advocated two-way communication and leadership that enabled others. However, the
relationship was reversed for presidents who were leaving or
had left office for whom directive leadership and one-way communication were associated with resource increases. Resource
increases were also associated with presidents who evaluated
themselves based on institutional outcomes rather than using
either constituent satisfaction or both outcomes and constituent satisfaction. Resources were more likely to increase on campuses with presidents not using adaptive strategy than on those
with presidents who did, and on campuses whose presidents used
interpretive strategy than on those whose presidents did not.

Relationships Between Measures of Campus Change

In addition to considering the relationship between institutions,
presidents, and change, it was also possible to assess the extent
to which the five measures of change — researcher assessments,
changes seen by faculty, discrepancies in faculty-president ratings, campus stress level, and total resource change — were related to each other and to constituent support. Relating each

of the five changes to the others and to constituent support yielded fifteen paired comparisons. Of these, only three had correlation coefficients of .30 or higher.

The highest correlation (+ .69) was between faculty and researcher perceptions of change, suggesting either that both interpreted the same data in much the same way, or that the assessments of the researchers were in part dependent on what faculty said about institutional change. The next highest (− .41) was between total resource change and institutional stress, indicating that as resources declined, stress increased. The third relationship (+ .34) was between faculty perceptions of change and discrepancies between faculty and presidential perceptions; as faculty saw the institution worsening, the discrepancy between their perceptions of change and those of the president (who was more likely to believe that the campus was improving) increased. These relationships were based on all thirty-two institutions. But even when only the twenty-one institutions with stable presidents were considered, the relationships between the five change measures and constituent support remained essentially the same.

The most interesting outcome, of course, was not that three correlations were .30 or higher, but that 12 were below that level. Changes in resource levels, for example, did not appear related to the nature of campus changes as seen by faculty, or to constituent support. Researcher assessments of campus change were not associated with campus stress levels. With few exceptions, measures of institutional change and constituent support appeared to be independent of each other.

While changes of various kinds may be seen as increasing institutional effectiveness (for example, there might be general agreement that it would be good if researchers saw a campus as improved, if faculty saw it as improved, if there were no discrepancies in presidential-faculty assessments, if stress were neither too high nor too low, and if resources increased), each of these changes may tap into somewhat different dimensions of organizational functioning. This is consistent with Cameron's (1978) finding that effectiveness is a multidomain construct, and that effectiveness in one domain may not necessarily be related to effectiveness in another.

What does this mean for the study of presidential leadership? If leadership makes a difference, it should be reflected in measurable organizational change. Let us assume that the five kinds of organizational change studied by the ILP, while severely limited in scope, were representative of the kinds of changes that could be plausibly related to leadership. These five changes were not only for the most part unrelated but may in fact have been incompatible, so that, as Cameron found in studying effectiveness, positive changes in one dimension could be achieved only at the cost of negative changes in another. This suggests that research that attempts to assess leadership effectiveness by relating presidential behavior to any single dimension of organizational change will be misleading. Studies using a *single* measure, such as ratings of reputation or some presumed outcome of leadership such as improved morale, will be incomplete.

The Meaning of Leadership and Campus Change

This Resource has reviewed the relationship between 21 characteristics and personal and cognitive presidential characteristics, constituent support, and five different ways of looking at institutional changes and conditions. The findings are summarized in Tables 8, 9 and 10. These tables together display 125 cells. Results have been entered in the 44 cells for which the ILP findings suggested the possibility of a relationship.

Of the 42 cells in Table 8 that might show possible links between seven institutional factors, constituent support, and measures of presidential effectiveness, 14 offer evidence of relationships that may not have been due to chance. These links indicate that structural and historical factors related to organizational operation may affect what presidents can realistically hope to achieve. However, for the most part the relationships observed were modest in size, suggesting that they may not prohibit positive institutional outcomes but merely make them somewhat more difficult to achieve.

There are 41 cells in Table 9 that could have displayed links between seven personal characteristics of presidents, constituent support, and campus change; ten of them suggested the

Table 8. The Relationship Between Institutional Characteristics, Constituent Support, and Institutional Change.

Institutional Factors	First Year	Longitudinal				
	Constituent Support	Researcher Assessment	Changes Seen by Faculty	President-Faculty Discrepancy	Institutional Stress	Resource Change
Bargaining or nonbargaining	Bargaining = low			Nonbargaining = low		Bargaining = decrease
System or nonsystem	System = low			Nonsystem = low		
Crisis or noncrisis		Crisis = improve	Noncrisis = worsen		Crisis = high	Crisis = decrease
Type: university, state college, independent college, or community college		State college = improve		Independent = none		State college = decrease
Control: public, private, or religious						
Wealth	Moderate = low					
Size						Small = decrease

Table 9. The Relationship Between Personal
Characteristics, Constituent Support, and Institutional Change.

| | First Year | | Longitudinal | | | |
Leader Characteristics	Constituent Support	Researcher Assessment	Changes Seen by Faculty	President-Faculty Discrepancy	Institutional Stress	Resource Change
Tenure: new or old	Old = low	New = improved	new = improved		Old = low	
Selection: inside or outside			Inside = worse			Inside = decrease
Previous presidencies: yes or no						
Faculty status: yes or no				Faculty = none		Faculty = decrease
Academic vice president: yes or no				AVP = none		
Gender: male or female				Male = none		
Constituent support: high, mixed, or low						

Table 10. The Relationship Between Cognitive Characteristics, Constituent Support, and Institutional Change

Cognitive Characteristics	First Year		Longitudinal			
	Constituent Support	Researcher Assessment	Changes Seen by Faculty	President-Faculty Discrepancy	Institutional Stress	Resource Change
Observed complexity: high, medium, or low	Low complexity = low					
Avowed strategy: linear, adaptive, or interpretive	Linear = low			Linear high	Linear = high Adaptive = low Interpretive = low	Adaptive = increase Interpretive = increase
Communications: one-way or two-way				One-way = high	One-way = low One-way = high	One-way = decrease
Orientation: Directive or Enabling				Directive = high	Directive = high Directive = low	Directive = decrease
Self-assessment: outcomes or constituent reaction		Both = improved	Both = improved	Both = low	Outcomes = high Outcomes = low	Outcomes = increase
Search: Passive or Active		Active = improved		Active = low		
Intuition: Yes or No						

existence of potentially interesting relationships. While most of these were modest in size, four were associated with presidential tenure. Whether a president was new or old appeared to be one of the most important factors potentially influencing institutional change. A major surprise was that constituent support, as determined during the first-year visit, did not appear to be related to any change seen at the time of the second visit. It was also interesting that experiences often considered to be important for presidential success, such as previous teaching background or service as academic vice president, did not appear related to campus changes. Research in other settings (Bettin and Kennedy, 1990) has indicated that positions previously held and the degree of relevant experience may be significant predictors of leader performance. The absence of such a relationship in this study may mean that academic experience is not required for a successful presidency, that presidents may gain their academic experience in other ways, or that selection processes function to select individuals with academic sensibilities even if they have not previously filled these particular roles.

Of the 42 potential connections between 7 cognitive factors, constituent support, and measures of institutional change in Table 10, 18 appear to reflect some kind of relationship. Of these cognitive characteristics, the most promising for further consideration were the potential negative consequences for constituent support of using linear strategy and the potential positive effects on constituent support of using cognitive complexity and interpretive strategy. Other cognitive characteristics, such as processes of communication and self-assessment, may also have a modest effect.

RESOURCE D

Publications of
the Institutional
Leadership Project

Books and Monographs

Bensimon, E. M., and Neumann, A. *Reconceptualizing Leadership: Teams and Teamwork in Higher Education.* Baltimore: Johns Hopkins University Press, forthcoming.

Bensimon, E. M., Neumann, A., and Birnbaum, R. *Making Sense of Administrative Leadership: The "L" Word in Higher Education.* ASHE/ERIC Higher Education Report. Washington, DC: Association for the Study of Higher Education, 1989.

Birnbaum, R. *How Colleges Work: The Cybernetics of Academic Organization and Leadership.* San Francisco: Jossey-Bass, 1988.

Birnbaum, R. (ed.). *Sharing Governance: The Role of Senates and Joint Committees in Academic Decision Making.* San Francisco: Jossey-Bass, 1991.

Birnbaum, R. *How Academic Leadership Works: Understanding Success and Failure in the College Presidency.* San Francisco: Jossey-Bass, 1992.

Fujita, E. M. "What Is a Good College President?: How Leaders are Judged by Constituents." Unpublished Ed.D. dissertation, Teachers College, Columbia University, 1990.

Note: Publications distributed by the Center for Higher Education and Leadership were originally published by its predecessor, the National Center for Postsecondary Governance and Finance.

Lathrop, J. J. "Sharing Leadership: The Nature of Relationships Between Presidents and Chief Academic Officers in Colleges and Universities." Unpublished Ed.D. dissertation, Teachers College, Columbia University, 1990.

Articles, Chapters, and Research Reports

Bensimon, E. M. "The Discovery Stage of Presidential Succession." College Park, Md.: Center for Higher Education Governance and Leadership, Report OP 87:15, 1987.

Bensimon, E. M. "A Feminist Reinterpretation of Presidents' Definitions of Leadership." *Peabody Journal of Education,* 1989, *66,* 143–156.

Bensimon, E. M. "Five Approaches to Think About: Lessons Learned from Experienced Presidents." In American Association for Higher Education, *On Assuming a College or University Presidency: Lessons and Advice from the Field,* Washington, D.C.: American Association for Higher Education, 1989.

Bensimon, E. M. "How Do Higher Education Leaders Define Quality?" Foreword to E. M Bensimon (ed.), *Quality in the Academy: Proceedings from a National Symposium.* College Park, Md.: Center for Higher Education Governance and Leadership, Report OP 89:3, 1989.

Bensimon, E. M. "The Meaning of 'Good Presidential Leadership': A Frame Analysis." *Review of Higher Education,* 1989, *12,* 107–123.

Bensimon, E. M. "The New President and Understanding the Campus as a Culture." In W. G. Tierney (ed.), *Assessing Academic Climates and Cultures.* New Directions for Institutional Research, no. 68. San Francisco: Jossey-Bass, 1990.

Bensimon, E. M. "Viewing the Presidency: Perceptual Congruence Between Presidents and Leaders on Their Campuses." *The Leadership Quarterly,* 1990, *1,* 71–90.

Bensimon, E. M. "How College Presidents Use Their Administrative Groups: 'Real' and 'Illusory' Teams." *Journal for Higher Education Management,* 1991, *7,* 35–51.

Bensimon, E. M. "The Presidency and Leadership: Alternatives to Charisma." In J. A. Sturnick, C. Tisinger, and J.

Milley (eds.), *Women at the Helm: Pathfinding Presidents of State Colleges and Universities.* Washington, D.C.: American Association of State Colleges and Universities, 1991.

Bensimon, E. M. "The Social Process Through Which Faculty Shape the Image of a New President." *Journal of Higher Education,* 1991, *62,* 637–660.

Bensimon, E. M. "New Presidents' Initial Actions: Transactional and Transformational Leadership." *Journal for Higher Education Management,* in press.

Birnbaum, R. "Leadership and Learning: The College President as Intuitive Scientist." *Review of Higher Education,* 1986, *9,* 381–395.

Birnbaum, R. "When College Presidents Are Wrong: The Effects of Knowledge Structures and Judgmental Heuristics on Administrative Inferences." College Park, Md.: Center for Higher Education Governance and Leadership, Report OP 87:6, 1987.

Birnbaum, R. "Administrative Commitments and Minority Enrollments: College Presidents' Goals for Quality and Access." *Review of Higher Education,* 1988, *11,* 435–457.

Birnbaum, R. "Individual Preferences and Organizational Goals: Consistency and Diversity in the Futures Desired by Campus Leaders." *Review of Higher Education,* 1988, *12,* 17–30.

Birnbaum, R. "Presidential Searches and the Discovery of Organizational Goals." *Journal of Higher Education,* 1988, *59,* 489–509.

Birnbaum, R. "The Reality and Illusion of Community College Leadership." In J. Eaton (ed.), *Colleges of Choice: The Enabling Impact of the Community College.* New York: American Council on Education/Macmillan, 1988.

Birnbaum, R. "The Cybernetic University: Toward an Integration of Governance Theories." *Higher Education,* 1989, *18,* 239–253.

Birnbaum, R. "The Implicit Leadership Theories of College and University Presidents." *Review of Higher Education,* 1989, *12,* 125–136.

Birnbaum, R. "The Latent Organizational Functions of the Academic Senate: Why Senates Do Not Work but Will Not Go Away." *Journal of Higher Education,* 1989, *60,* 423–443.

Birnbaum, R. "Leadership and Followership: The Cybernetics of University Governance." In J. H. Schuster and L. Miller (eds.), *Governing Tomorrow's Campus: Perspectives and Agendas.* Washington, DC: American Council on Education/Macmillan, 1989.

Birnbaum, R. "Presidential Succession and Institutional Functioning in Higher Education." *Journal of Higher Education,* 1989, *60,* 123–135.

Birnbaum, R. "The Quality Cube: How College Presidents Assess Excellence." In E. M. Bensimon (ed.), *Quality in the Academy: Proceedings from a National Symposium.* College Park, Md.: Center for Higher Education Governance and Leadership, Report OP 89:3, 1989.

Birnbaum, R. "Responsibility Without Authority: The Impossible Job of the College President." In J. Smart (ed.), *Higher Education: Handbook of Theory and Research.* Vol. 5. New York: Agathon Press, 1989.

Birnbaum, R. "How'm I Doin'?: How College Presidents Assess Their Effectiveness." *The Leadership Quarterly,* 1990, *1,* 25–39.

Birnbaum, R. "How to Improve Campus Productivity." *AGB Reports,* 1991, *33*(3), 6–11.

Birnbaum, R. "Why It's Difficult to Improve Productivity." *AGB Reports,* 1991, *33*(2), 6–11.

Birnbaum, R. "Will You Love Me in December as You Do in May?: Why Experienced College Presidents Lose Faculty Support." *Journal of Higher Education,* 1992, *63,* 1–25.

Birnbaum, R. "The Constraints to Campus Productivity." In J. Meyerson and R. E. Anderson (eds.), *Productivity and Higher Education.* Princeton, N.J.: Peterson's, forthcoming.

Birnbaum, R., Bensimon, E. M., and Neumann, A. "Leadership in Higher Education: A Multidimensional Approach." *Review of Higher Education,* 1989, *12,* 101–105.

Chaffee, E. E. "Leadership in Higher Education: Variations on a Theme." *Review of Higher Education,* 1989, *12,* 167–175.

Fujita, E. M. "The Evaluation of College Presidents: Dimensions Used by Campus Leaders." College Park, Md.: Center for Higher Education Governance and Leadership, Report OP 90:16, 1990.

Hollander, E. P. "College and University Leadership from a

Social-Psychological Perspective: A Transactional View." College Park, Md.: Center for Higher Education Governance and Leadership, Report OP 87:11, 1987.

Kellerman, B. "The Politics of Leadership in America: Implications for Higher Education in the Late 20th Century." College Park, Md.: Center for Higher Education Governance and Leadership, Report OP 88:1, 1988.

Lee, B. A. "Leadership and Campus Governance." In R. Birnbaum (ed.), *Faculty in Governance: The Role of Senates and Joint Committees in Academic Decision Making.* New Directions for Higher Education, no. 75. San Francisco: Jossey-Bass, 1991.

Neumann, A. "Strategic Leadership: The Changing Orientations of College Presidents." *Review of Higher Education,* 1989, *12,* 137–151.

Neumann, A. "Making Mistakes: Error and Learning in the College Presidency." *Journal of Higher Education,* 1990, *61,* 386–407.

Neumann, A. "On the Making of 'Good Times' and 'Hard Times': The Social Construction of Resource Stress." College Park, Md.: Center for Higher Education Governance and Leadership, Report OP 90:18, 1990.

Neumann, A. "Defining 'Good Faculty Leadership.'" *Thought and Action,* 1991, *7,* 45–60.

Neumann, A. "The Thinking Team: Toward a Cognitive Model of Administrative Teamwork in Higher Education." *Journal of Higher Education,* 1991, *62,* 485–513.

Neumann, A. "College Planning: A Cultural Perspective." *Journal for Higher Education Management* (in press).

Neumann, A. "Colleges Under Pressure: Budgeting, Presidential Competence and Faculty Uncertainty." *Leadership Quarterly,* in press.

Neumann, A. "Double Vision: Experiencing Institutional Life During Times of Stability." *Review of Higher Education,* in press.

Neumann, A., and Bensimon, E. M. "Constructing the Presidency: College Presidents' Images of Their Leadership Roles, a Comparative Study." *Journal of Higher Education,* 1990, *61,* 678–701.

Tierney, W. G. "Symbolism and Presidential Perceptions of Leadership." *Review of Higher Education,* 1989, *12,* 153–166.

References

Ashford, S. J. "Self Assessments in Organizations: A Literature Review and Integrative Model." *Research in Organizational Behavior,* 1989, *11,* 133–174.

Avolio, B. J., and Yammarino, F. J. "Operationalizing Charismatic Leadership Using a Level-of-Analysis Framework." *The Leadership Quarterly,* 1990, *1,* 193–208.

Bass, B. M. *Leadership and Performance Beyond Expectation.* New York: Free Press, 1985.

Bass, B. M. *Bass & Stogdill's Handbook of Leadership: Theory, Research, and Managerial Applications.* (3rd ed.) New York: Free Press, 1990.

Bennis, W., and Nanus, B. *Leaders: The Strategies for Taking Charge.* New York: HarperCollins, 1985.

Bensimon, E. M. "The Discovery Stage of Presidential Succession." College Park, Md.: Center for Higher Education Governance and Leadership, Report OP 87:15, 1987.

Bensimon, E. M. "A Feminist Reinterpretation of Leadership." *Peabody Journal of Education,* 1989a, *66,* 143–156.

Bensimon, E. M. "Five Approaches to Think About: Lessons Learned From Experienced Presidents." In American Association for Higher Education, *On Assuming a College or University Presidency: Lessons and Advice from the Field.* Washington, D.C.: American Association for Higher Education, 1989b.

Bensimon, E. M. "The Meaning of 'Good Presidential Leadership': A Frame Analysis." *Review of Higher Education,* 1989c, *12,* 107–123.

Bensimon, E. M. "The New President and Understanding the Campus as a Culture." In W. G. Tierney (ed.), *Assessing Academic Climates and Cultures.* New Directions for Institutional Research, no. 68. San Francisco: Jossey-Bass, 1990a.

Bensimon, E. M. "Viewing the Presidency: Perceptual Congruence Between Presidents and Leaders on Their Campuses." *The Leadership Quarterly,* 1990b, *1,* 71–90.

Bensimon, E. M. "How College Presidents Use Their Administrative Groups: 'Real' and 'Illusory' Teams." *Journal for Higher Education Management,* 1991a, *7,* 35–51.

Bensimon, E. M. "The Social Processes Through Which Faculty Shape the Image of a New President." *Journal of Higher Education,* 1991b, *62,* 637–660.

Bensimon, E. M. "New Presidents' Initial Actions: Transactional and Transformational Leadership." *Journal for Higher Education Management,* in press.

Bensimon, E. M., Neumann, A., and Birnbaum, R. *Making Sense of Administrative Leadership: The "L" Word in Higher Education.* ASHE/ERIC Higher Education Report No. 1. Washington, D.C.: Association for the Study of Higher Education, 1989.

Berliner, D. C. *The Development of Expertise in Pedagogy.* Charles W. Hunt Memorial Lecture, American Association of Colleges for Teacher Education, New Orleans, 1988.

Bettin, P. J., and Kennedy, J. K., Jr. "Leadership Experience and Leader Performance: Some Empirical Support as Well." *Leadership Quarterly,* 1990, *1,* 219–228.

Birnbaum, R. "Leadership and Learning: The College President as Intuitive Scientist." *Review of Higher Education,* 1986, *9,* 381–395.

Birnbaum, R. *How Colleges Work: The Cybernetics of Academic Organization and Leadership.* San Francisco: Jossey-Bass, 1988a.

Birnbaum, R. "Presidential Searches and the Discovery of Organizational Goals." *Journal of Higher Education,* 1988b, *59:* 489–509.

Birnbaum, R. "The Implicit Leadership Theories of College and University Presidents." *Review of Higher Education,* 1989a, *12,* 125–136.

Birnbaum, R. "The Latent Organizational Functions of the Academic Senate." *Journal of Higher Education,* 1989b, *60,* 423–443.

Birnbaum, R. "Presidential Succession and Institutional Functioning in Higher Education." *Journal of Higher Education,* 1989c, *60,* 123–135.

Birnbaum, R. "The Quality Cube: How College Presidents Assess Excellence." In E. M. Bensimon (ed.), *Quality in the Academy: Proceedings from a National Symposium.* College Park, Md.: Center for Higher Education Governance and Leadership, Report OP 89:3, 1989d.

Birnbaum, R. "Responsibility Without Authority: The Impossible Job of the College President." In J. Smart (ed.), *Higher Education: Handbook of Theory and Research.* Vol. 5. New York: Agathon Press, 1989e.

Birnbaum, R. "'How'm I Doin'?: How College Presidents Assess Their Effectiveness." *The Leadership Quarterly,* 1990a, *1,* 25–39.

Birnbaum, R. "Will You Love Me in December as You Do in May?: Why Experienced College Presidents Lose Faculty Support." *Journal of Higher Education,* 1992, *63,* 1–25.

Birnbaum, R., Bensimon, E. M., and Neumann, A. "Leadership in Higher Education: A Multidimensional Approach." *Review of Higher Education,* 1989, *12,* 101–105.

Blau, P. M. *Organization of Academic Work.* New York: John Wiley and Sons, 1973.

Bolman, L. G., and Deal, T. E. *Modern Approaches to Understanding and Managing Organizations.* San Francisco: Jossey-Bass, 1984.

Bolman, L. G., and Deal. T. E. *Reframing Organizations: Artistry, Choice and Leadership.* San Francisco: Jossey-Bass, 1991.

Burns, J. M. *Leadership.* New York: HarperCollins, 1978.

Cameron, K. S. "Measuring Organizational Effectiveness in Institutions of Higher Education." *Administrative Science Quarterly,* 1978, *23,* 604–629.

Cameron, K. S. "The Enigma of Organizational Effectiveness."

In D. Baugher (ed.), *Measuring Effectiveness.* New Directions for Program Evaluation, no. 11. San Francisco: Jossey-Bass, 1981.

Cameron, K. S. "A Study of Organizational Effectiveness and its Predictors." *Management Science,* 1986, *32,* 87–112.

Chaffee, E. E. "Successful Strategic Management in Small Private Colleges." *Journal of Higher Education,* 1984, *55,* 212–241.

Chaffee, E. E. "Three Models of Strategy." *Academy of Management Review,* 1985, *10,* 89–98.

Chaffee, E. E. "Leadership in Higher Education: Variations on a Theme." *Review of Higher Education,* 1989a, *12,* 167–175.

Chaffee, E. E. "Strategy and Effectiveness in Systems of Higher Education." In J. Smart (ed.), *Higher Education: Handbook of Theory and Research.* Vol. 5. New York: Agathon Press, 1989b.

Chaffee, E. E., and Tierney, W. G. *Collegiate Culture and Leadership Strategies.* Washington, D.C.: American Council on Education/Macmillan, 1988.

Chait, R. P., Holland, T. P., and Taylor, B. E. *The Effective Board of Trustees.* New York: American Council on Education/Macmillan, 1991.

Cohen, M. D., and March, J. G. *Leadership and Ambiguity: The American College Presidency.* New York: McGraw-Hill, 1974.

Commission on Strengthening Presidential Leadership. *Presidents Make a Difference: Strengthening Leadership in Colleges and Universities.* Washington, D.C.: Association of Governing Boards of Universities and Colleges, 1984.

Conger, J. A., and Kanungo, R. N. "Behavioral Dimensions of Charismatic Leadership." In J. A. Conger, R. N. Kanungo, and Associates (eds.), *Charismatic Leadership: The Elusive Factor in Organizational Effectiveness.* San Francisco: Jossey-Bass, 1988.

Cyert, R. M. "Defining Leadership and Explicating the Process." *Nonprofit Management and Leadership,* 1990, *1,* 29–38.

Dill, D. D. "The Nature of Administrative Behavior in Higher Education." *Educational Administration Quarterly,* 1984, *20,* 69–99.

Feldman, J. M. "Beyond Attribution Theory: Cognitive Processes in Performance Appraisal." *Journal of Applied Psychology,* 1981, *66,* 127–148.

Feldman, J. M. "On the Difficulty of Learning from Experience." In H. P. Sims, Jr., D. A. Gioia, and Associates (eds.), *The Thinking Organization.* San Francisco: Jossey-Bass, 1986.

Finkelstein, S., and Hambrick, D. C. "Top-Management-Team Tenure and Organizational Outcomes: The Moderating Role of Managerial Discretion." *Administrative Science Quarterly,* 1990, *35,* 484–503.

Fisher, J. L. *Power of the Presidency.* New York: Macmillan, 1984.

Fisher, J. L., Tack, M. W., and Wheeler, K. J. *The Effective College President.* New York: American Council on Education/Macmillan, 1988.

French, J. R. P., Jr., and Raven, B. "The Bases of Social Power." In D. Cartwright and A. Zander (eds.), *Group Dynamics: Research and Theory.* New York: HarperCollins, 1968.

Fujita, E. M. "What Is a Good College President?: How Leaders Are Judged by Constituents." Unpublished Ed.D. dissertation, Teachers College, Columbia University, 1990.

Gardiner, J. J. "Building Leadership Teams." In M. F. Green (ed.). *Leaders for a New Era: Strategies for Higher Education.* New York: Macmillan, 1988.

Gardner, J. W. *On Leadership.* New York: Free Press, 1990.

Gilley, J. W., Fulmer, K. A., and Reithlingshoefer, S. J. *Searching for Academic Excellence: Twenty Colleges on the Move and Their Leaders.* New York: American Council on Education/Macmillan, 1986.

Glaser, R., and Chi, M.T.H. "Overview." In M.T.H. Chi, R. Glaser and M. J. Farr, (eds.), *The Nature of Expertise.* Hillsdale, N.J.: Erlbaum, 1988.

Goleman, D. "The Dark Side of Charisma." *The New York Times,* Apr. 1, 1990, F1.

Green, J., Levine, A., and Associates (eds.). *Opportunity in Adversity: How Colleges Can Succeed in Hard Times.* San Francisco: Jossey-Bass, 1985.

Green, M. F. *The American College President: A Contemporary Profile.* Washington, D.C.: American Council on Education, 1988a.

Green, M. F. "Toward a New Leadership Model." In M. F. Green (ed.)., *Leaders for a New Era: Strategies for Higher Education.* New York: Macmillan, 1988b.

Hodgkinson, C. *Educational Leadership: The Moral Art.* Albany, N.Y.: State University of New York Press, 1991.

Hogan, R., Raskin, R., and Fazzini, D. "The Dark Side of Charisma." In K. E. Clark, and M. B. Clark (eds.), *Measures of Leadership.* West Orange, N.J.: Leadership Library of America, 1990.

Hollander, E. P. "Leadership and Power." In G. Lindzey and E. Aronson (eds.), *The Handbook of Social Psychology.* (3rd ed.) New York: Random House, 1985.

Hollander, E. P. "College and University Leadership from a Social-Psychological Perspective: A Transactional View." College Park, Md.: Center for Higher Education Governance and Leadership, Report OP 87:11, 1987.

Johnson, E. J. "Expertise and Decision Under Uncertainty: Performance and Process." In M.T.H. Chi, R. Glaser, and M. J. Farr, (eds.), *The Nature of Expertise.* Hillsdale, N.J.: Erlbaum, 1988.

Johnson, G. W. "Shaping the Future of Higher Education." In American Association of State Colleges and Universities, *Shaping the Future of Higher Education: Presidential Leadership.* Washington, D.C.: American Association of State Colleges and Universities, 1990.

Kanter, R. M. *Men and Women of the Corporation.* New York: Basic Books, 1977.

Katz, R. "The Effects of Group Longevity on Project Communication and Performance." *Administrative Science Quarterly,* 1982, *27,* 81–104.

Kauffman, J. F. *At the Pleasure of the Board.* Washington, D.C.: American Council on Education, 1980.

Keller, G. *Academic Strategy: The Management Revolution in Higher Education.* Baltimore: Johns Hopkins University Press, 1983.

Kelley, R. E. "In Praise of Followers." *Harvard Business Review,* 1988, *66*(6), 142–148.

Kerr, C., and Gade, M. L. *The Many Lives of Academic Presidents: Time, Place and Character.* Washington, D.C.: Association of Governing Boards, 1986.

Kouzes, J. M., and Posner, B. Z. *The Leadership Challenge: How to Get Extraordinary Things Done in Organizations.* San Francisco: Jossey-Bass, 1987.

Kuh, G. D., and Whitt, E. J. *The Invisible Tapestry: Culture in American College and Universities.* ASHE-ERIC Higher Education Report, no. 1. Washington, D.C.: Association for the Study of Higher Education, 1988.

Lathrop, J. J. "Sharing Leadership: The Nature of Relationships Between Presidents and Chief Academic Officers in Colleges and Universities." Unpublished Ed.D. dissertation, Teachers College, Columbia University, 1990.

Leatherman, C. "Colleges Have More Female Presidents, But Questions Linger About Their Clout." *Chronicle of Higher Education,* Nov. 6, 1991, A19–A20.

Lee, B. A. "Leadership and Campus Governance." In R. Birnbaum (ed.), *Faculty in Governance: The Role of Senates and Joint Committees in Academic Decision Making.* New Directions for Higher Education, no. 75. San Francisco: Jossey-Bass, 1991.

Levitt, B. and March, J. G. "Organizational Learning." *Annual Review of Sociology,* 1988, *14,* 319–340.

Meindl, J. R., Ehrlich, S. B., and Dukerich, J. M. "The Romance of Leadership." *Administrative Science Quarterly,* 1985, *30,* 78–102.

Merriam-Webster. *Webster's Ninth New Collegiate Dictionary.* Springfield, Mass.: Merriam-Webster, 1988.

Meyer, J. W., and Rowan, B. "Institutionalized Organizations: Formal Structure as Myth and Ceremony." In J. W. Meyer and W. R. Scott (eds.), *Organizational Environments: Ritual and Rationality.* Newbury Park, Calif.: Sage, 1983.

Miles, M. B. and Huberman, A. M. *Qualitative Data Analysis.* Newbury Park, Calif.: Sage, 1984.

Mitroff, I. I. *Stakeholders of the Organizational Mind: Toward a New View of Organizational Policy Making.* San Francisco: Jossey-Bass, 1983.

Neumann, A. "Strategic Leadership: The Changing Orientations of College Presidents." *Review of Higher Education,* 1989, *12,* 137–151.

Neumann, A. "Making Mistakes: Error and Learning in the College Presidency." *Journal of Higher Education,* 1990, *61,* 386–407.

Neumann, A. "A Case Analysis of Collegiate Leadership and Cultural Change." Paper presented at the Annual Meeting of the American Educational Research Association, Apr. 1991a.

Neumann, A. "Defining 'Good Faculty Leadership.'" *Thought and Action,* 1991b, *7,* 45–60.

Neumann, A. 'The Thinking Team: Toward a Cognitive Model of Administrative Teamwork in Higher Education." *Journal of Higher Education,* 1991c, *62,* 485–513.

Neumann, A. "Colleges Under Pressure: Budgeting, Presidential Competence and Faculty Uncertainty." *Leadership Quarterly,* in press.

O'Reilly, C. A. III. "The Use of Information in Organizational Decision Making: A Model and Some Propositions." In L. L. Cummings and B. M. Staw (eds.), *Information and Cognition in Organizations.* Greenwich, Conn.: JAI Press, 1990.

Perlman, B., Gueths, J., and Weber, D. A. *The Academic Intrapreneur: Strategy, Innovation and Management in Higher Education.* New York: Praeger, 1988.

Pfeffer, J. "The Ambiguity of Leadership." *Academy of Management Review,* 1977, *2,* 104–112.

Pfeffer, J. "Management as Symbolic Action: The Creation and Maintenance of Organizational Paradigms." In L. Cummings and B. M. Staw (eds.), *Research in Organizational Behavior.* Vol. 3. Greenwich, Conn.: JAI Press, 1981.

Pfeffer, J. "Organizational Demography." In L. Cummings and B. M. Staw (eds.), *Research in Organizational Behavior.* Vol. 5. Greenwich, Conn.: JAI Press, 1983.

Pfeffer, J., and Salancik, G. R. *The External Control of Organizations: A Resource Dependence Perspective.* New York: HarperCollins, 1978.

Phillips, J. S., and Lord, R. G. "Causal Attributions and Perceptions of Leadership." *Organizational Behavior and Human Performance,* 1981, *28,* 143–163.

Pondy, L. R. "Leadership Is a Language Game." In M. W. McCall, Jr., and M. M. Lombardo (eds.), *Leadership: Where Else Can We Go?* Durham, N.C.: Duke University Press, 1978.

Rosener, J. B. "Ways Women Lead." *Harvard Business Review,* 1990, *68*(6), 119–125.

Roueche, J. E., Baker, G. A., and Rose, R. R. "Transformational Leaders in the Community College: The Best of the

Best." *American Association of Junior and Community College Journal,* 1988, *58,* 36–41.

Schein, E. H. *Organizational Culture and Leadership: A Dynamic View.* San Francisco: Jossey-Bass, 1985.

Scott, W. R. *Organizations: Rational, Natural, and Open Systems.* Englewood Cliffs, N.J.: Prentice-Hall, 1981.

Shavlik, D. L., and Touchton, J. G. "Women as Leaders." In M. F. Green (ed)., *Leaders for a New Era: Strategies for Higher Education.* New York: Macmillan, 1988.

Simon, H. A. "Making Management Decisions: The Role of Intuition and Emotion." *Academy of Management Executive,* 1987, *1*(1) 57–64.

Smircich, L., and Morgan, G. "Leadership: The Management of Meaning." *The Journal of Applied Behavioral Research,* 1982, *18,* 257–273.

Smith, P. B., and Peterson, M. F. *Leadership, Organizations and Culture: An Event Management Model.* London: Sage, 1988.

Streufert, S., and Swezey, R. W. *Complexity, Managers, and Organizations.* Orlando, Fla.: Academic Press, 1986.

Taylor, B. E., Chait, R. P., and Holland, T. P. "Trustee Motivation and Board Effectiveness." *Nonprofit Voluntary Sector Quarterly,* 1991, *20,* 207–224.

Van der Veer, G. "Cognitive Complexity and the Career Achievement of Higher Education Administrators." Unpublished Ph.D. dissertation, University of Maryland, College Park, 1991.

Vaughan, G. B. *The Community College Presidency.* New York: American Council on Education/Macmillan, 1986.

Vaughan, G. B. *Leadership in Transition: The Community College Presidency.* New York: American Council on Education/Macmillan, 1989.

Walker, D. E. "Goodbye, Mr. President, and Good Luck." *Educational Record,* 1977, *58*(1) 53–58.

Walker, D. E. *The Effective Administrator: A Practical Approach to Problem Solving, Decision Making, and Campus Leadership.* San Francisco: Jossey-Bass, 1979.

Weick, K. E. *The Social Psychology of Organizing.* (2nd ed.) Reading, Mass.: Addison-Wesley, 1979.

Weick, K. E. "Cognitive Processes in Organizations." In L. L. Cummings and B. M. Staw (eds.), *Information and Cognition in Organizations*. Greenwich, Conn.: JAI Press, 1990.

Whetten, D. A., and Cameron, K. S. "Administrative Effectiveness in Higher Education." *Review of Higher Education*, 1985, *9*, 35–49.

Yukl, G. A. *Leadership in Organizations*. Englewood Cliffs, N.J.: Prentice-Hall, 1981.

Index